D1333316

PETER ALLISS'S
100
GREATEST
GOLFERS

PETER ALLISS'S
100
GREATEST
GOLFERS

WITH MICHAEL HOBBS

Macdonald
Queen Anne Press

A *Queen Anne Press* BOOK

© Peter Alliss and Michael Hobbs 1989

First published in Great Britain in 1989 by
Queen Anne Press, a division of
Macdonald & Co (Publishers) Ltd
6th Floor
Headway House
66–73 Shoe Lane
London EC4P 4AB

A member of Maxwell Pergamon Publishing Corporation plc

Jacket photographs Walter Hagen Hulton Picture Company
Seve Ballesteros All-Sport

British Library Cataloguing in Publication Data
Alliss, Peter, *1931–*
    Peter Alliss's 100 greatest golfers.
    1. Golf. – Biographies
    I. Title   II. Hobbs, Michael, *1934–*
796.352′092′2

ISBN 0-356-17863-3

Typeset, printed and bound by Butler & Tanner Limited in Great Britain

Picture Credits

All-Sport: 19, 55, 74, 77, 151, 177, 205, 223, 235; Associated Press: 106, 107, 192, 195,
207; Bettmann News Photos: 23, 27, 32, 64, 73, 83, 87, 116, 133, 134, 178, 179, 202,
211, 220, 250; Peter Dazeley: back flap, 9, 33, 38, 47, 60, 80, 98, 105, 123, 174, 204,
244, 255; Michael Hobbs Collection: 13, 15, 16, 31, 35, 49, 51, 86, 89, 91, 111, 141,
185, 188, 226; Hulton-Deutsch Collection: 61, 67, 85, 102, 103, 147, 156, 170, 181,
191, 194, 198, 214, 225, 242; Macdonald/Aldus Archive: 138, 247; Mansell Collection:
36; Bob Thomas Sports Photography: 24, 29, 41, 44, 52, 57, 79, 93, 95, 109, 114, 117,
128, 144, 145, 148, 153, 156, 161, 165, 167, 172, 178, 179, 184, 201, 217, 222, 232, 240,
249; S & G Photo Library: 100 120, 131, 229, 252, 253; Phil Sheldon: 11, 69, 125, 136,
154, 163, 173, 209, 223, 236

Colour photographs by Phil Sheldon except for Gary Player, Tony Jacklin, Greg
Norman, Calvin Peete, Curtis Strange, Ian Woosnam, Sam Snead, Jan Stephenson
(All-Sport), Young Tom Morris and Old Tom Morris (Michael Hobbs Collection)
and Laura Davies (Bob Thomas)

CONTENTS

INTRODUCTION

The figure 100 is a magic one in so many sports: the man who wins the Olympic 100 metres becomes acclaimed as 'the fastest man on earth'; in football, to win 100 caps is somehow much better than 'only' 99. This is even more clear-cut in cricket: a score of 99 will be forgotten by the record keepers unless it was scored in a desperately tight situation. In golf no one is at all keen to score a century. On the contrary, the first target for a newcomer to the game is to get below that figure. Few golfers can aspire to win that number of tournaments; the only professionals to get there are the Argentine, Roberto de Vicenzo, Sam Snead of the United States and Gary Player of South Africa.

In golf, which events you win counts a great deal more than how many. By far the most important are the four major championships. Oldest of these is the Open Championship which began at Prestwick in 1860. It was followed in 1895 by the US Open. Twenty-one years later came the US PGA Championship, for many years a matchplay event and perhaps later a little diminished in stature because it changed over to the usual 72-hole strokeplay format. The newcomer is the Masters, which is not actually a championship of anything, the creation of the great Bobby Jones and Clifford Roberts, enhanced by being played on the same course every year and featuring those do-or-die shots over water on the second nine. I have given great weight to winning these events but I have also included very successful tournament players who failed to win a major. For example, fine though Andy North's achievement was in twice winning the US Open I could not give him a place ahead of such superb golfers as Isao Aoki or Graham Marsh, who have no majors on their records but far more tournament victories.

Making comparisons across the years has been enormously difficult. The modern fairway is considerably smoother than nineteenth and early twentieth century putting greens. Bunkers are filled with carefully selected and graded sand where once they were a wilderness, unraked, full of weeds and unloved. The changes in equipment have been equally dramatic. Swinging a hickory-shafted club or looking at a thin-bladed iron club you might well wonder how the players of old managed to cope at all. The steel shaft made the game a great deal easier, while the ball improves from year to year. I was at my longest from the tee in the early 1950s, but the modern ball gives me almost the same distance I had 40 years ago. This means that comparisons of scores are almost meaningless.

Few players have been near certain winners every time they played and then for only a few years. Young Tom Morris, Harry Vardon for two or three, Bobby Jones, Byron Nelson and Ben Hogan are the only clear examples. Even so, I had not the slightest doubt in selecting my first 50 or so golfers: they chose themselves. There was much burning of the midnight oil over the remaining places, however.

I have tried not to be prejudiced by nationality and I am confident that I have succeeded. The different generations were far more of a problem. Many would argue that there are far more good players around today than there were in the past and I would agree. But I believe that I have chosen the 100 golfers who are best at *winning*. You will find that I have missed out a number of players who have made their million and won virtually nothing. Their names will not last, even if their bank managers are happy.

When I had completed my list of 100 I gave some thought to the Allisses, my father Percy and I, and felt we deserved to be in. Either of us could have beaten the last few on my list most days of the week.

Like father like son, they say, and our playing achievements and abilities are certainly very similar. Neither of us, some said, could putt it into a bucket; both were superb long iron players; both thought golf a simple game (except for the putting!); both ranked as high as any British player during our respective peak years. And both failed to win the Open Championship. Aye, there's the rub. As Open champions we would have found immortality, joining names on the trophy like Tom Kidd, Jack Burns and Hugh Kirkaldy, while the names of individual tournaments tend to disappear as sponsors lose enthusiasm. For all time, you are 'Open Champion, 1877 or 2007' or whatever.

In my extreme youth, winning the Open Championship didn't seem to matter all that much. I met a few Open champions and, with the exception of Henry Cotton, it had meant surprisingly little in their lives. They made no great sums of money as a result and fame was strictly temporary. They went back to their clubs to try to persuade members to try a new set of golf clubs or buy two balls instead of one.

My father came close to winning. In Sarazen's year (1932) he felt he might well have won by a street. He was at a peak in his long game but, alas, in a trough on the greens. He tied 4th that year. At Carnoustie, the year before, he had come 3rd with a ball out of bounds on the very last hole. He was also 4th in both 1928 and 1929 and 5th in 1936.

I was less successful, three 8th places are the best on my record (but I was just 4 behind in 1954), but with over 20 major tournament wins I have the edge. He, however, won the British Professional Matchplay Championship in both 1933 and 1937 – an event which then ranked just behind the Open Championship in status. Both of us were good performers in the Ryder Cup and I was in the two-man England team pairing in the World Cup ten times.

Nowadays, I am active in golf course design in partnership with Clive Clark, and television work. My tournament career is 20 years away. People sometimes come up to me and say 'And did you ever play the game as a pro, Mr Alliss?'. Well, now they know!

AMY ALCOTT

Is your notion of a typical woman's golf swing one that goes well past the horizontal so as to give enough 'room' to develop clubhead speed on the way back to the ball? It's quite true that many women do swing rather like this, including some of the top touring professionals of both the United States and Europe. But not Amy Alcott. She has a backswing

Amy Alcott (1956–) USA, was born in Kansas City, Missouri. One of the most prolific winners on the US LPGA Tour. She won the US Women's Open in 1980, the Peter Jackson Classic in 1979 and the Dinah Shore Invitational in 1983.

One of the most athletic of women golfers, Amy Alcott delivers great clubhead speed from an unusually short backswing

not very much longer than the legendary Doug Sanders, who, it was said, could swing inside a telephone box. It takes remarkable athleticism for a woman to be able to develop so much clubhead speed so quickly.

A superb iron player, Alcott had only a short amateur career, with the highlight being her 1973 US Junior Championship. She turned professional in 1975 and was immediately successful. She won the third event she entered – the Orange Blossom Classic – which is considered to be an LPGA record (although, if one thinks back to the very beginnings of the Tour, someone must have won the first event!).

In 1975 she finished 15th in the money list and, up to the end of 1988, has never been worse than 17th. Her victory sequence is even more impressive: she has had at least one tournament win every year apart from 1987. Her best years were 1979, 1980 and 1984 with four victories in each season.

Her money-winning achievements have been highly consistent. Between 1975 and 1988 she has had only three years out of the top ten and has twice been 3rd and twice 4th. Still in her early thirties, she is a player who might emerge one year to sweep all before her as, for example, Mickey Wright, Nancy Lopez and Pat Bradley have done before.

Amy has one particular aim in mind as regards the major championships: to win the LPGA title would make her the second player, after Pat Bradley, to win all four. Her career total of 27 Tour victories means she is close to automatic entry to the LPGA Hall of Fame, and her money winnings of more than $2 million place her in the top four.

Her greatest performance, very appropriately, came in the 1980 Women's Open which she dominated all the way through. Beginning with a round of 70, she followed with scores of 70, 68 and 72 which, temporarily, set a scoring record for the championship. She won by nine strokes. You can't argue with that.

ISAO AOKI

No Japanese player has yet won a major championship and one reason for this is that they concentrate their efforts on home tournaments. The Japan Tour pays rich rewards. It is not worth competing on either the US or European Tours tournament by tournament. Neither does any Japanese player attend, for example, the Open Championship or the US Open year after year. Isao Aoki and Tsuneyuki Nakajima are the only players from Japan to make frequent forays overseas.

Aoki has had considerable success: in 1978, he won the World Matchplay Championship at Wentworth and five years later the European Open at Sunningdale. At Muirfield, in 1980, his 63 in the third round equalled the lowest single round ever shot in the Open Championship and he finished 12th. He had been well up the previous year also finishing 7th as he had in 1978. That year, at St Andrews, he had a chance of winning. After two rounds, he was tied for the lead and at that point four strokes better than the eventual champion, Jack Nicklaus.

*Isao Aoki
(1942–   )
Japan, was born in Abiko, Chiba.
One of very few Japanese players to become well-known outside his own country.*

Aoki lines up a putt. He is the most successful Japanese player on the international circuit, with wins in America, Britain and Australia

Aoki was still in contention after the third round, only one behind, but a 73 on the final day wasn't good enough to clinch the title.

Aoki's greatest performance in a major came in the 1980 US Open. By chance, he was paired with Jack Nicklaus throughout and had three consecutive rounds of 68 at Baltusrol to tie for the lead against Nicklaus's rounds of 63, 71, 70. Their 54-hole totals broke the previous record. Aoki did little wrong in the final round but Nicklaus was unbeatable, especially over the last nine. Aoki broke the previous scoring record for the four rounds but his 70 to Nicklaus's 68 meant he came 2nd.

In Japan, Aoki had won 52 events by the end of 1987. The biggest prize, the Japan Open, long eluded him but he eventually won it in 1983, after four times being runner-up, and repeated his success in 1987. He has won the Japan Matchplay Championship five times and in early 1989 became the first Japanese player to win an Australian tournament.

Aoki hit one of the most spectacular shots ever in the 1983 Hawaiian Open. Playing the last, a par 4, he needed a birdie to tie Jack Renner. Aoki's second shot found the left rough and from there he holed out from 128 yards and became the first Japanese golfer to win on the US Tour.

Aoki was a late developer; he turned professional in 1964 but it was seven years before his first victory. Rather like the young Gary Player, the general opinion was that Aoki would never make a top golfer. His technique was all against him. While two of the basics are a full shoulder turn and a driving leg action, Aoki relies on a wristy flick at the ball. It seems to have taken him until his thirties to make it work. There was never much doubt about his putting. Though this is every bit as unorthodox as his long game – wristy with the toe of the centreshaft putter high in the air – it has sometimes looked as though he doesn't know how to miss.

TOMMY ARMOUR

Tommy Armour was the last player, born and bred in Scotland, to win the Open Championship, although he did not become a great player until well after he had emigrated to the USA. By that time, however, he had already made quite a reputation for himself in Britain. As an amateur he was runner-up in the 1919 Irish Open, won the 1920 French Amateur Championship and lost a play-off for the Canadian Open in the same year. In 1921, he played for Britain in the first international match with the USA at Hoylake. Not long after this, Armour moved to the United States and, helped by a recommendation from Walter Hagen, was given a job worth $10,000 a year as social secretary of the Westchester-Biltmore Club.

His golf improving all the time, Armour turned professional in 1924 and won his first tournament the following year. He became truly

Thomas Dickson Armour (1895–1968) Scotland and USA, was born in Edinburgh. Though famous for the quality of his iron play, his driving was probably superior to it. He won the Open Championship in 1931, the US Open in 1927 and the US PGA in 1930.

When his peak playing days were over, Tommy Armour became renowned as a raconteur, teacher and a best-selling golf author

successful in 1927, however, when he won several tournaments, one of which was the US Open. This was a remarkable victory; the likely winner, Harry Cooper, was already in the clubhouse as Armour struggled to the turn in 39 and then had two double bogeys on the next three holes. He had to be two under par on the remaining holes to tie. On the last tee, he needed a birdie to tie. He played a 3-iron to about a dozen feet and holed the putt. The play-off was close but Armour again birdied the last, which gave him a fine victory.

About a week later, he showed he had a flair for publicity. Playing a par 3 which he thought required a draw from the tee, Armour overdid it again and again. His marker wrote down 21 in the end. Armour claimed that he had actually taken 23. 'Open champion takes 21' was still good enough to make the headlines and he was on his way to becoming one of the characters of the game.

Tournament successes continued to come his way. His next major win resulted from defeating Gene Sarazen in the final of the US PGA. Armour's sights, however, had long been set on the Open Championship and victory came in 1931 at Carnoustie. Armour's 71 on the final afternoon was a very fine round but this championship was thrown away by both José Jurado from Argentina and my father Percy who both had disastrous finishes.

By this time Armour was in his late thirties, but he had other fields left to conquer. His playing career was probably ended by the 'yips', a term that Armour invented. Another of his creations was slow play; Armour was just as interested in the conversation as in the golf as he went round the course. When he got to his ball, he had to waggle the club a great deal before he could bring himself to hit the ball. He was, he said, waiting until he 'felt ready' and with Armour suffering from the yips, this took an age on the greens. To criticism, however, he had an effective retort which was, 'Who said the game should be played fast? The tempo of the game has slowed down as efficiency has increased.' From the point of view of the golfers, he would go on to point out, 'Tournament players have nothing else to do when they've finished'.

Eventually, Armour decided to concentrate on teaching. One way to convince his pupils of the value of the advice they were getting was to charge them heavily. His fees, first $50 then $100 an hour, were probably the highest in America! After morning lessons in Florida, Armour would take his pupils out onto the golf course and fleece them all over again. His students were often hopelessly confused by the complicated betting systems he thought up. Later on, he wrote one of the most successful golf instruction books ever – *How to Play Your Best Golf All the Time*. The core message was to hit like hell with the right hand.

JOHN BALL

John Ball was part of the great flowering of Hoylake amateur golf and was more revered at his home club than any – including the equally great Harold Hilton. John Ball grew up with the Royal Liverpool Golf Club which was founded in 1869 and was soon its best player, a title never clearly taken away from him, despite the achievements of Hilton.

*John Ball
(1861–1940)
England, born in Hoylake, Cheshire.
The first Englishman to win the Open Championship and winner of more major championships than any other British player. He won the Amateur Championship in 1888, 1890, 1892, 1894, 1899, 1907, 1910 and 1912 and the Open Championship in 1890.*

Hoylake's two Open champions: Harold Hilton (left) and John Ball

A rare action shot of John Ball playing for England against Robert Maxwell of Scotland (standing left of centre)

Ball was one of the few great players who succeeded despite not being highly rated as a putter. His swing was regarded as being of great beauty (Bernard Darwin preferred it to Bobby Jones') though this is difficult to believe from the many photographs that have survived of him in action and the fact that he gripped the club in the palm of his right hand, in what used to be the traditional manner. In other ways, however, he was an evolutionary player. Few at the beginning of Ball's career felt it necessary, or correct, to hold onto the club firmly at the top of the backswing, but Ball did. He also, before Taylor and Vardon, showed that it was not unrealistic to try to hit the long iron and woods right up to the flag.

Ball played in the first Amateur Championship of all, held at Hoylake in 1885, and made his first appearance in the Open Championship in 1878 at Prestwick at the age of 16. Ball was up with the leaders after the first round of the 12 holes. He held on very well to finish in a tie for 4th. Ball's attention centred on amateur golf, like most of his contemporaries, and he did not play in the Open again until 1890, a year in which he already held the amateur title. He was one of 39 competitors and quite highly fancied to win. Out towards the end of the field, he found his 82 put him just a stroke behind the leader, Andrew Kirkaldy, after the first of the two rounds of Prestwick, a course since increased to 18 holes. Kirkaldy then collapsed to an 89 and Ball found that with four to play he could afford 20 strokes over holes that had taken him 18 in the morning. He won by three.

Observers were impressed by his long straight driving and the fact that his play to the greens left him with no great strain on his putting. His score-cards show that he played far more steadily than his closest rivals – the reigning champion, Willie Park jnr, for example, began his defence 6, 3, 8, 6, and Andrew Kirkaldy only managed scores as good as 4 on four holes. Ball, on the other hand, played both nines – which were of equal difficulty – in 41. Ball competed regularly in the Open after triumphantly becoming the first Englishman and first amateur to win. In 1892 he tied for 2nd place but could not get as close again.

The Amateur Championship was the scene of his greatest achievements, which not even Harold Hilton and Michael Bonallack have come close to rivalling. The title must have been almost as difficult to win as the Open. Anyone can suddenly produce a brilliant round, even against the best player of the day, and all the best amateurs stayed in the game. Today, the majority turn professional if they think themselves good enough.

Ball might well have won a couple more titles if the championship had been started a few years earlier but even so his record of eight wins is quite likely to stand for ever. He was past 50 at the time of his last success in 1912 and reached the last 16 as late as 1921 when he thought that he might win again if the wind blew fiercely.

SEVERIANO BALLESTEROS

*Severiano Ballesteros
(1957–   )
Spain, was born in Pedrena,
Santander.*

*The greatest figure in the
game of golf today. He won
the Open Championship in
1979, 1984 and 1988 and the
US Masters in 1980 and
1983.*

In the end, there are only a few comparisons we can make between generations. You can't expect any more of a player than that he beat his contemporaries. But perhaps you can compare their variety of talents, as seen by observers and remarked on by the players themselves. Very often, they are outstanding in a few areas of the game but have weaknesses as well – sometimes very pronounced ones. There was, for example, the bad short putting of Harry Vardon, the wildness of Walter Hagen, or the limitations of Jack Nicklaus around the greens.

In comparison, Ballesteros seems to me to have all the talents that go to make up the complete golfer. Few have more length from the tee and no one the speed of hand that can tear the ball from the most difficult lies. When controlled – not sheer – power is most needed for the shot to the green, no one in modern golf is more likely to hit a long or mid-iron close to the flag. When the Spaniard misses the green, he is the acknowledged genius at manipulating the ball. Most good professionals can play a few standard shots; Ballesteros seems able to invent new ones to fit the situation. To complete this rough outline of what golf is about, he is, as he once modestly said, 'the best bunker player', a deft chipper and a very good putter indeed.

Are there no weaknesses then? Once there were plenty of wild shots, which caused certain Americans to give him the soubriquet 'the car park champion' after his Lytham Open Championship win in 1979. Though that drive among cars was not into a public car park but an area just off the course allotted to BBC vehicles, Ballesteros certainly hit few fairways and the occasional drive did bend almost sideways. Even then, however, these weren't simple bad shots but more the deliberate draw or fade which, overdone, became a hook or a slice.

Ballesteros went along with the jokes. They did his dashing image no harm. In recent years, however, he has been quite concerned to stress that he has become a straight hitter and points out that long hitters are bound to get into trouble more often than their gentler colleagues do. The angles mean you have to be straighter.

Seve first appeared from nowhere at Royal Birkdale in 1976. There had been a whisper in the golfing world that there was a new talent on the rise in Spain and he had been noticed by the great Argentine Roberto de Vicenzo. To most, though, he was an entirely new name at the top of the leader board after an opening round of 69. The press wanted to know if the young Spaniard, still only 19, could do it again. Not if the wind got up, he thought. Everyone thought Seve was one of those brief comets who so often lead a major championship on the first day. It wasn't so: Ballesteros produced another 69, despite a poor first nine, to lead the field by two. Though he took 73 the third day, he kept his two-stroke lead. But the fairy tale ending didn't come.

It's in the bag! Seve has just chipped stone-dead from the fringe of the last green at Lytham during the 1988 Open. Nick Price was left with an impossibly long putt to tie, and failed

Johnny Miller outplayed him and Ballesteros managed to get 2nd place only because he finished well, after scattering strokes to the wind. But Seve was on his way. He had a steady flow of international victories over the next year or two. He won several events in mainland Europe and Britain, Japan, New Zealand, Kenya and, early in 1978, came his first US win in the Greater Greensboro Open; before his 21st birthday, he was a star on the world stage.

In 1979 came his first major championship at Lytham, where he played a similar brand of golf to Birkdale. This time there was no Miller finishing with a 66. The third round leader and US Open champion, Hale Irwin, withered away and Seve won by three strokes from Ben Crenshaw and Jack Nicklaus. The key to his victory was his second round 65, approached by no one else that championship. Seve reached the turn in 33 – not an outstanding score on Lytham's easier first nine – and finished his round with scores of 3, 3, 4, 3, 3 on holes whose true par that windy day was 4, 5, 4, 5, 4.

For Americans who had scoffed at his driving, Ballesteros had the answer at Augusta the following year, 1980. He began with a 66 to share the lead, followed with a 69 to lead by three and then left the field far behind with a 68 that put him seven strokes ahead. A record aggregate for the Masters was in sight. During the fourth round, Seve increased his lead to an embarrassing ten strokes at one stage but the dropping of five strokes on three holes, the 11th to the 13th, with two shots in water, kept his margin within bounds – four strokes.

Majors are becoming harder to win. Ballesteros nowadays must produce not just four good rounds but at least one supercharged spell as well. He did this in the 1983 Masters, opening up in the final round birdie, eagle, par, birdie and reaching the turn in 31. This time he was unfaltering over the last nine until he reached the last green. With his second shot through the back, Seve totally misjudged his chip but then compensated by holing his next attempt. It all added to the Ballesteros legend.

In 1984 came his second Open Championship success which was the result of steady play as his scores of 69, 68, 70 and 69 testify. He putted beautifully throughout yet very little dropped. If at Lytham his avowed strategy was to hit the ball to parts of the course which gave him the best line in for the shots to the green (and never mind the rough), at St Andrews he claims to have aimed his tee shots to areas where no bunkers lay in wait. Mostly, this meant playing his tee shots left, safe enough on the Old Course but usually the wrong side from which to hit the greens. The strategy worked, however, and there was a supercharged bit at the end: at the feared 17th, a 4 which may be the hardest par in world golf, Ballesteros drove safely left into the rough, which leaves an almost impossible shot to hit and hold the green. Yet he succeeded and then, while Tom Watson faltered behind him, birdied the last – and the emotions flowed.

By the time of Ballesteros's next victory in a major, many were wondering if a flaw had become clear in his make-up as he had thrown a few away. In 1986, he had the Masters in his grasp but let Nicklaus in when he hit a very bad 4-iron into water on the 15th at Augusta and followed with three-putts at the 17th. The next year, he three-putted to go out of the play-off with Greg Norman and Larry Mize and struck a very bad putt near the end which lost him his chance in the US Open.

The answer came at Lytham in 1988: after a blistering start the round was held together for a 67. Then came that classic last round finale involving the title-holder, Nick Faldo, and Nick Price. Price did nothing wrong – round in 68, starting two ahead – and Ballesteros shot a 65. It was little short of the Nicklaus/Watson duel at Turnberry in 1977 for excitement.

Of course, major championships are not the whole story. Ballesteros has been the most powerful influence in turning the Ryder Cup matches upside down. His presence has meant that the Europeans believe that they have the world's best player; he has produced the results as well, at The Belfry in 1985 and outstandingly at Muirfield Village in 1987.

In tournaments worldwide, Ballesteros usually starts favourite and his record is perhaps even better than in the majors. By the end of 1988, he had 56 wins, 42 of these on the European Tour. Although Seve has victories in the United States to his credit, many would like to see him mount an all-out assault on the US Tour. In recent years, he has restricted his appearances to the majors and a very few other tournaments. Perhaps we need to see a dominant season in the US from him – and a US Open or two would do no harm to his reputation either.

JIM BARNES

James M. Barnes
(1887–1966)
USA, was born at Lelant,
near St Ives, Cornwall,
England.
One of many golfing
emigrants from Britain to
build successful careers in the
USA. He won the 1925
Open Championship, the
1921 US Open and the US
PGA in 1916 and 1919.

One of the most famous collapses in the history of the Open Championship was that of Macdonald Smith. He went into the final round at Prestwick in 1925 looking almost certain to win (a 78 would have done it) but took 82. Jim Barnes was the man who benefited and so became one of only eight to win all three of the major championships. Almost certainly he would have won the Masters also had the event been invented when he was at his peak.

Barnes began his golf career as an assistant at the West Cornwall Golf Club at Lelant, but went off to seek his fortune in San Francisco in his late teens. He first began to be noticed as a US Open contender just before the First World War and was 4th in 1913 (year of Francis Ouimet's famous victory) and in 1915 and came 3rd in 1916. In the same year he had his first great success, beating another emigrant, Jock Hutchison, in the final the first year that the US PGA Championship was played.

Because of the war there was a gap until 1919, when Barnes won again, beating another emigrant Fred McLeod in the final. How good a matchplayer he was can be seen from the fact that he reached two more finals, in 1921 and 1924, but was beaten 3 and 2 and 2 up by Walter Hagen, the first American born and bred golfer to become the leading figure in world golf.

Perhaps Barnes's greatest triumph, however, was in the 1921 US Open. He started off with a 69 to lead and drew away from the field round by round. He eventually won by nine strokes from Walter Hagen and Fred McLeod. He was the first and, so far, the only golfer to have the trophy presented to him by a US president.

In terms of his major championship successes in his ten peak years, Barnes ranks very high among his contemporaries but his fame didn't last as long. There are very few stories told about either Barnes the man or his victories. He was quiet rather than charismatic and played his golf in almost complete silence with a blade of clover or grass often between his teeth. Though very tall golfers are now commonplace, Barnes was the first of well over six feet (he was six feet four inches) to become a golfer of high quality. It always used to be the theory that a height of around five feet eight to five feet nine inches was the ideal. Very tall golfers tend to lack co-ordination and have the obvious disadvantage that they stand further away from the ball.

Barnes is thought to have won 17 other tournaments in the United States. He took up US citizenship but liked to revisit Britain and presented a trophy to West Cornwall which is still competed for. He did not play in the first international between Britain and America in 1921 but played for the US in the first match for the Ryder Cup in 1926. Thereafter, he was ruled out because of his English birth.

OPPOSITE: *Jim Barnes shows*
an interested Walter Hagen
(centre) and friend how to putt
with a driver

and in a heat-wave at that. Even so, Bolt was cross when he saw his age given in the local press as 49 when he was ten years younger. 'It was just a typographical error, Tommy', the reporter exclaimed. 'Typographical error, my ass', Bolt shouted. 'It was a perfect 4 and a perfect 9'!

Bolt was a late starter in tournament golf and, because of that swing, he lasted a long time. Bolt didn't go on the Tour until he was 32 in 1950 and quickly thought he was better than anyone else. He first won in 1951 and featured in the top 60 (players who didn't have to pre-qualify for tournaments) most years from 1951 through to 1967, when he was almost 50 years old.

Bolt won 15 US Tour events and almost added another major, the 1952 Masters. With four holes to play, he was level with the eventual champion, Sam Snead. Bolt three-putted three of those last four greens, which is not altogether surprising as he was a poor putter and a winner only because of the splendour of the rest of his game.

If the Seniors' Tour had been invented by the late 1960s, Tommy would have made a killing. As it was, he won the National Seniors Association Open five times in a row from 1968 to 1972 and in 1969 took the US Seniors. Later the same year he went on to win the World Seniors, beating John Panton on the 39th hole. In the late 1970s he played the occasional tournament by invitation on the European Tour and did well. He also won the Australian Seniors in both 1978 and 1979.

MICHAEL BONALLACK

In terms of competitive results, there is no doubt at all that Michael Bonallack, now secretary of the R and A, is one of the three great British amateur golfers. Although his record is perhaps inferior to John Ball and Harold Hilton's, he was almost certainly far better on and around the greens. I am not prepared to go further than that in making comparisons with men born three generations apart; each beat the best golfers of their times and dominated the amateur game.

If Bonallack had been born a dozen or so years later, he would almost certainly have turned professional and, with the best short game in British golf, would have been highly successful. Though most golfers make the change because of the possibilities of wealth from tournament

Michael Francis Bonallack (1934–)
England, was born at Chigwell in Essex. Though sometimes suffering difficulties in the long game, Bonallack was an outstanding short-game player and putter. He won the Amateur Championship in 1961, 1965, 1968, 1969 and 1970.

Michael Bonallack's record-breaking run of three consecutive Amateur Championship wins is an achievement unmatched even by John Ball and Harold Hilton

winnings, sponsorship and endorsements, the very best players naturally want to compete against the best which means playing on the US or European Tours. In Bonallack's case, there was something else to consider: he didn't think he was good enough until he was 'too old'. Although Bonallack began to win important amateur events when still in his teens, he didn't move into a dominant position in the amateur game until after his mid–twenties. Then his record became phenomenal. No one else has ever won the Amateur Championship three times in a row as Bonallack did in the years 1968–70. No one in modern times has approached his total of five victories. His five English Amateur Championships are a record, as are his four English Strokeplay titles. One of those English Amateur wins illustrates his abilities in the short game: playing in the 1963 final at Burnham and Berrow against Alan Thirlwell, he managed to get down in two after missing 22 greens and eventually won by 4 and 3.

Bonallack also produced one of the most phenomenal scoring bursts ever seen, in the 1968 final at Ganton. In the morning he was round in 61 and went on to win by 12 and 11 – another record. Bonallack didn't rate his own swing highly, claiming it was more suited to shovelling coal, and went to great lengths to improve it during the winter of 1967/8. He emerged to have his greatest year, winning the Amateur Championship, the English Amateur and Strokeplay Championships, being leading amateur in the Open and taking a host of lesser titles.

By this time his swing was certainly good enough but what impressed me the most was his putting. His method was to spread his legs wide and crouch down over the ball, his nose almost touching the top of the putter shaft. Then, he seemed to will the ball into the hole.

Bonallack was an automatic choice for the Walker Cup teams from 1957 to 1973 and was one of the select few to have captained a winning team (in 1971). He also appeared in the Eisenhower Trophy in all seven events in the period 1960–72 and had a similar record for the matches against Europe. Bonallack went on to take a leading role in the administration of both amateur and professional golf before becoming secretary of the R and A in 1983.

JULIUS BOROS

Julius Boros was a very late starter in tournament golf. He was 30 when he turned professional and gave up accountancy. He was immediately successful and might have won the US Open in his first year. He finished well up the field, his chances of winning destroyed by one bad round.

He was back again the next year and this time, 1951, was 4th behind Ben Hogan at the feared Oakland Hills. Next year at Northwood it was Hogan's turn to give way, with Boros, after Hogan had led him by four strokes at 36 holes, cruising home four strokes ahead of Porky Oliver.

Boros' new fame meant that people sat up and took notice of how he played the game. Most had never seen golf look easier: he just walked up slowly to his ball, shuffled his feet into position and, without a pause, swung. That swing was also something special. Bobby Jones once wrote that 'No one ever swung a golf club too slowly'. Jones followed his own dictum but everyone could see how he whipped the clubhead into the ball. Boros seemed to be slow the whole way back and there wasn't very much difference in the pace of the downswing. Or so he made it look.

On the greens, Boros was correspondingly quick, allowing himself to set up and steal a quick glance along the line before he sent his putt on its way. However, bear in mind that golfers play the way they think suits their game. The agonisingly deliberate player believes that he will score very much worse if he speeds up. Nicklaus, for instance, when he used to spend an age motionless before he committed himself to the putting stroke, used to reply to criticism by saying 'I just have to wait till I feel ready'. Boros was by no means as relaxed as he looked; his fear was that if he didn't play quickly, he might freeze over the ball for minutes on end.

The next time Boros won the US Open he was rather taken by surprise. In his morning round on the final day in 1963 he had taken 76 when already well off the lead. The 72 in the afternoon was certainly better and probably good enough to place well up the field. He went off to get all his gear together ready for a quick departure. Actually only two other players scored as low as 72 in either round on the final day.

Julius's high aggregate of 293, nine over par, began to look good as no one beat it. Palmer, the halfway leader, took 77 in his third round and had no thoughts of winning as he played the last. However, he holed a short putt for his 4 and a round of 74. Behind them, a young Tour player whose game didn't last, Jacky Cupit, took a two-stroke advantage into the 17th – and then double-bogeyed it. A par for him at the last meant a three-way play-off.

Julius Nicholas Boros (1920–   ) USA, was born in Fairfield, Connecticut.
One of the great examples of how a player's game can last if he has a relaxed, rhythmical swing. He won the US Open in 1952 and 1963 and the US PGA in 1968.

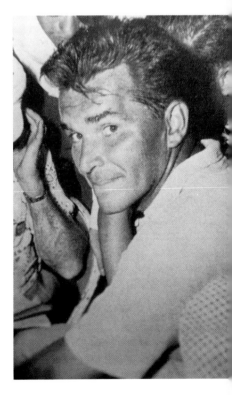

Julius Boros wins the first of his two US Opens at Northwood, Texas, in 1952 by four strokes from Porky Oliver. Ben Hogan was another stroke behind

The next day the high winds, which had been the main cause of the poor scoring, were gone. Boros quickly went three strokes into the lead and reached the turn in 33. A little later Palmer was finally out of the contest in a once famous incident. At the 11th, he hooked his ball into the woods and it lodged in the top of a rotten tree stump. Palmer decided to play the ball as it lay instead of dropping away under penalty; this was a mistake and he ended with a 7 on this par 4. He put in a magnificent finish with birdies at three of the last four holes – but much too late. Boros finished with a 70, six strokes better than Palmer, and beat Cupit by three.

At 43, Boros was the second oldest US Open champion at the time. (Floyd became the oldest in 1986.) Five years later, Boros became the oldest winner of a major championship when he won the US PGA at the age of 48. Much later, at 55, he threatened Sam Snead's status as the oldest winner of a US Tour event; Snead had won at 52, Boros shot a 65 in the last round of the 1975 Westchester Classic to tie with Gene Littler, a mere youth of 45. Alas, Julius lost the sudden death play-off. Afterwards the press enquired about his retirement plans: 'Retire to what?', he replied. 'All I do now is play golf and fish.'

Boros won 18 US Tour events and made more than $1 million, mostly in the days before prize money was so substantial.

PAT BRADLEY

Pat Bradley's record of winning six events ranked as majors on the LPGA Tour in the 1980s, is unequalled. (As an aside, for non-American readers, though perhaps for them also, I should explain the complexities of the ranking system the US LPGA have for major tournaments. The LPGA Championship and the US Women's Open will surely cause no difficulty but some have disappeared from the calendar – the Title-holders, for instance, and the Peter Jackson Classic, which later became the Du Maurier.)

Patricia Bradley
(1951–   )
USA, was born in Westford, Massachusetts.
One of few players to have a year of almost total dominance. She won the Peter Jackson Classic in 1980, the US Women's Open in 1981, the Du Maurier Classic in 1985 and 1986, the Nabisco Dinah Shore in 1986 and the LPGA Championship in 1986.

Pat Bradley: one of the dominant players on the LPGA Tour today

33

Pat Bradley's amateur career made her a name to be reckoned with mainly in the New England region of the United States. There she won the New Hampshire state title in 1967 and 1969, the New England in 1972 and 1973 and the Massachusetts in 1972. By 1974 she was on the LPGA Tour and by 1976 was one of the leading players. That year, she won her first LPGA tournament and moved right up the money list to 6th place. She had her first win in Australia the previous year — the Colgate Far East Open.

For the next dozen years, she remained a key player. From 1976 to 1986 she was only once placed worse than 8th in the money lists and had seven years where she finished in the top four. In this period she was once 1st, twice 2nd and twice 3rd. Such consistency meant that Pat Bradley had won nearly $2\frac{1}{2}$ million by the end of 1987 and was well ahead of JoAnne Carner as the leading money-winner of all time. In that same year, she also extended her run of $100,000 seasons to a record ten.

Her biggest year, however, was 1986 when she came close to a grand slam of the four major titles. Only the US Open eluded her, in which she finished at 5th place. She broke all the money-winning records; she was quickest to $200,000, $300,000 and $400,000 and her season's total of nearly $\frac{1}{2}$ million was a record.

Her finest victory, perhaps, was in the 1981 US Open. Here she was six behind the leaders after two rounds with a start of 71 and 76. She then improved with a 69 and closed devastatingly with a 66. Her aggregate of 279 was yet another record and she was also the most ever under par.

By the end of 1988 her career victory total stood at 22. Ill health was the main reason for a very poor season with only about $16,000 banked but she can surely expect a few more years at or near the top of the golfing ladder.

JAMES BRAID

James Braid's record in the Open Championship illustrates that he was the dominant member of the so-called Great Triumvirate of Vardon, Taylor and himself during the first ten years or so of this century. Braid, though of very much the same age, took longer to reach his peak than the others. Legend has it that he first became a force to be reckoned with when he awoke one day at 17 to find that he had become a long driver overnight. Braid could never quite account for why it happened. We can only speculate that a driver of just the ideal weight, lie and length of shaft for him was responsible. Perhaps, on the other hand an unconscious change of technique made the difference. The result, however, was clear; Braid was a much longer hitter than Taylor and usually could outdrive Harry Vardon also. More importantly, he could tear a ball out of tight and buried lies to the wonder of onlookers. All this, of course, hardly made Braid a champion; for several years in the second half of the 1890s, he lacked the precision of the other two and was an unreliable putter.

In rather the same way that James Braid's driving had changed instantaneously, so did his putting. This time, as has happened so often since, it was a putter which made the difference. In the 1900 Open, Braid had another good finish – he came 3rd. He had come in tied for 5th in 1899, 2nd in 1897 and 6th in 1896. But he couldn't win. Shortly after the 1900 event he tried one of the aluminium-headed putters made by Mills of Sunderland which were becoming popular and his confidence grew. Rapidly, Braid became an outstanding putter and his first championship followed, at Muirfield in 1901, where Harry Vardon and J.H. Taylor followed him home, three and four strokes behind. Oddly, Braid began with a hook out of bounds from the 1st tee (the Muirfield layout was very different at the time) and reached the turn in what might seem a disastrous 43. However, he managed to salvage 79 for his first round and a 76 then gave him a narrow lead. His 74 to follow equalled the lowest round in the championship and his final 80 was good enough for victory.

If these scores seem high, you can knock off seven or eight strokes to take account of modern improvements in playing equipment, the ball and the manicured modern golf course. Even so, Braid, Vardon and Taylor were sending scores tumbling. Quickly, Taylor's winning 326 aggregate at Sandwich in 1894 began to seem laughable. All his rounds had been in the 80s; just a few years later, an average of well under 80 was needed to win, and rounds under 70 were played in the Open from time to time.

Braid next won at St Andrews in 1905 by five and again in 1906 at Muirfield by an emphatic four strokes. His greatest performance was still to come, however, when he shattered the championship record at

James Braid (1870–1950) Scotland, was born at Earlsferry in Fife. Won the Open Championship in 1901, 1905, 1906, 1908 and 1910. He was a long driver and an excellent putter at his peak.

A St Andrews Laddie

Duncan

Duncan Driving

Mr John Graham Jun:

Among those present

Braid playing Push Cleek.

Kirkaldy

Vardon Putting

J. H. Taylor's Mashie Pitch.

Herd

as the sign that he ought to turn professional. In fact, he kept on working in a bank for several more years, not turning professional until he was sure he could make a living at the game, in 1960. He first competed in Europe in 1961 but joined the US scene the following year and won the Houston Open in 1963. This was the year that he had a far more significant victory in the Open Championship at Royal Lytham. Arnold Palmer, having won in both 1961 and 1962, had just lost a play-off for the US Open and was hot favourite. Instead, it was another American, Phil Rodgers, who went into an early lead with rounds of 67 and 68. Charles lay five behind, unnoticed, perhaps the way he prefers it. He made it all up, and more, in the third round when Rodgers took 73 to the New Zealander's 66. In fact this should have been Jack Nicklaus's first Open Championship; he finished by three-putting the 15th and also dropped shots on the last two holes. Charles tied with Phil Rodgers and went on to win the 36-hole play-off to become the first and only New Zealander and left-hander to win any major championship. Charles was also responsible for Open Championship play-offs being reduced from 36 holes; he quietly enquired whether 18 weren't enough.

Though Charles won no more majors, he did finish 2nd in the Open twice – in 1968 and 1969 – was twice 3rd in the US Open (1964 and 1970) and came 2nd in the 1968 US PGA. For a time he made his home in the USA and had five career wins, including the 1968 Canadian Open, on that Tour. Later he based himself in South Africa and concentrated on Europe, scene of some of his finest achievements. In 1969, he won the World Matchplay and the John Player Classic and Dunlop Masters consecutively in 1972. Now into his fifties, Charles is very successful on the US Seniors' Tour. Ironically, he is still the best left-hander in the world and, just to keep the record straight, isn't a natural left-hander at all. He does everything else right-handed!

OPPOSITE: *Bob Charles's remarkable putting won him the World Matchplay in 1969. He is one of the greatest putters of all time and the best of left-handed golfers*

NEIL COLES

Neil Coles
(1934–   )
England, was born in London.
One of the most successful
British tournament players in
the period 1960 to 1977.

Although well into his fifties, Neil Coles still has the game to compete with the young lions when he has a good week. Only an occasional European Tour competitor in recent years, Coles still managed to win nearly £50,000 in 1987 which, because of the rise in prize money, was his best year financially in some 30 years of tournament golf. While we are on the subject of money, it is worth mentioning that Coles was the first player to reach £200,000 in European career money-winnings and not so long ago stood at 2nd in the all-time list. Today of course, he is not even in the top 20. In 1963, he was leading money-winner, with a princely £3,742 and again in 1970, this time with £13,528. In the period 1961 to 1980, he was never out of the top dozen and was 12 times in the top half dozen, which shows astonishing consistency.

Neil has been nearly as consistent as a tournament winner. He took his first title in 1956 but didn't really get into his stride until the 1960s. Apart from a barren spell in the years 1967–9, he won every year up to 1974 and usually more than once. His last European victory came in 1982, the Sanyo Open in Spain when he had reached the age of 48. It was his 28th on the European Tour and he has also won two other international events.

Coles must wish that there was a full Seniors' Tour in Europe as he would surely be enormously successful. No doubt it will come but perhaps too late for him: even for Seniors, the younger the better. However, in the limited golf for the over-fifties, Coles was, as expected, highly successful, winning the PGA Seniors' Championship as soon as he qualified in 1985 and going on to record wins in 1986 and 1987. He also won the first Seniors' British Open in 1987. Why then has he made no real attempt to compete on the US Seniors' Tour? The reason is his acute dislike of air travel, in the first place. Secondly, Coles might very well not fancy spending a long period of time away from his hobbies (woodwork, cars and 'Do-It-Yourself') and home. For past Ryder Cup matches, he used to travel by sea when the rest of the team flew to the United States. This fear of flying also prevented Neil from trying the full US Tour to any extent though in the years when he was at his best few British golfers were ambitious enough or had the necessary confidence for the experiment.

One of Coles's greatest regrets must be that he never managed to win the Open Championship, partly due, perhaps, to another of his dislikes – links golf. His best performances saw him finish equal 3rd in 1961, and in 1973 – thanks to an excellent final round of 66 – he tied for 2nd place with Johnny Miller, three strokes behind the champion Tom Weiskopf. With a round to go, he also had a good chance in the Carnoustie championship of 1975. A round of 70 would have done it but Coles took 74 to finish back in 7th place. Among his most prestigious victories are the 1966 Dunlop Masters, the 1976 PGA Championship and the PGA Matchplay which he won three times. For many years, Coles remained the only British player to reach the final of the World Matchplay at Wentworth. He did this in 1964, the first year of the event, by beating Tony Lema and Bruce Devlin, but then lost a close contest by 2 and 1 to Arnold Palmer.

Despite possessing a grip that would make many golfers prone to hook, consistency has been Coles's great forte and, once he was past the first flush of youthful club-throwing and general bad temper, he has always kept himself in tight control. Coles was never an outstanding putter but made up for that with his great abilities around the green.

Neil Coles was at the top of British golf for many years. Only the Open Championship escaped him, perhaps because he prefers to play inland courses

GLENNA COLLETT

Glenna Collett (later Vare) (1903–89) USA, was born in New Haven, Connecticut. The greatest figure in US women's golf in the 1920s and 1930s. She won the US Women's Championship in 1922, 1925, 1928, 1929, 1930 and 1935.

Only the great JoAnne Carner, with five victories, has managed to approach Glenna Collett's record in the premier American women's amateur event. Collett was also twice a losing finalist and won the Eastern Championship seven times and the North and South on six occasions.

Glenna's first enthusiasm was baseball, and she didn't try her hand at golf until she was 14. She found her mother to be very encouraging: golf was acceptable, baseball unladylike. In a few years, she had developed a swing which hit the ball record distances yet she did this with grace, rhythm and balance, not sheer strength.

She first made the headlines when she beat the visiting British star, Cecil Leitch. The very next year Glenna won her first American Championship and went on to win the Canadian title in 1923 and 1924. In the American Championship of 1924 she was knocked out at the semi-final stage in what must be one of the most unlucky finishes ever. Playing the last, Glenna was one up against her opponent, tennis star Mary K. Browne, who hit a tree with her second shot. She won the hole when her ball ricochetted onto the green. On the first extra hole, Miss Browne was just as lucky; her long putt hit Glenna's ball and changed course – into the hole. It was fortunate that Glenna Collett was a graceful loser, though losing was not an experience she often faced in her peak years.

Once established as the best American player, Glenna decided to attempt to win the British Ladies' title. If she could overcome Cecil Leitch and Joyce Wethered, there could be no doubt who was the best player in the world. She made her first entry in 1925 at Troon but came up against Joyce Wethered in the third round and went down by 3 and 1. However, she had the consolation of crossing the Channel and winning the French Ladies'.

In 1929, she fought through to the final of the British Ladies'. Alas, she faced Joyce Wethered again who had retired from the game but had entered the competition mainly because she was attracted by the idea of a week's golf at St Andrews. Glenna made a brilliant start this time. Out in 34 she was five up. However, Joyce Wethered first fought back and then dominated, eventually winning by 3 and 1.

In 1930 Glenna Collett again got through to the final of the British Ladies', and this time there was no Joyce Wethered. Instead, she faced 19-year-old Diana Fishwick (later mother of BBC golf commentator Bruce Critchley). 'What a lark!' said Diana – and went on to win by 4 and 3. A few years later, in 1935, Glenna Collett played in her last US final where her opponent was the 17-year-old Patty Berg. Glenna won 3 and 2.

She played for the US Curtis Cup team from the first match, in

1932, up to 1948 and was non-playing captain in 1950. She would probably be recognised as one of the greatest champions of all time had she managed to win the British title just once but that championship resisted American attacks until the arrival of Babe Zaharias after the Second World War.

HENRY COTTON

*Thomas Henry Cotton
(1907–87)
England, was born in Holmes
Chapel, Cheshire.
Regarded as the true successor
to Vardon, Braid and Taylor.
He won the Open
Championship in 1934,
1937 and 1948.*

Throughout the development of British professional golf, players have come into the game from working class backgrounds. After all, there wasn't very much money in the game, unless you were a star of the Taylor, Vardon and Braid calibre, so successful amateurs had no incentive to turn professional. The rules of amateur status were fairly loose and playing excellence brought its own rewards. People used to urge, early this century, that the distinction between amateur and professional should be abolished: the amateurs were profiting from the game though they didn't play it as well as the professionals did. All the while, however, the gap in playing standards was widening. In the 1890s, the Open Championship was won by amateurs three times but Bobby Jones is the only amateur to have done so since, and the story is much the same in the US Open.

With Cotton's background, he might well have become an amateur. He was born into the middle class, the son of an iron founder, and had a public school education at Alleyn's School in Dulwich. He decided he wanted to be a professional golfer so his father took him to J.H. Taylor for an opinion on his talents. Taylor noted Henry's concentration and thought that he might go far.

In later years, Cotton earned the reputation of being the first British golfer to practise until the hands bled and the back refused to straighten. Was this so? It's very hard to tell; we hear no tales of those who give their all but fail to make a mark. As a result of all this practice, observers tended to say that Cotton was not a 'natural' golfer and that he had 'manufactured' his swing. Yet one of the most remarkable things about Cotton's career is how quickly he made a reputation at a time when most professionals didn't seem to mature until the age of 30 or so. Cotton, on the other hand, was seen as a future star almost from the moment of his first tournament appearance. He was equally successful as a club professional. His first job was as an assistant at Fulwell but he quickly moved on to Rye, where he had more opportunities to play and practise. By the age of 19 he was full professional at Langley Park. This was a phenomenal rate of progress by any standard.

But for Cotton a club job was just part of his route to success. In 1926 he made his first Open Championship appearance and the following year played a very good first 36 holes at St Andrews and eventually came in 8th. The championship now became his goal but the Americans were winning it as a matter of course. Having reached the Matchplay Championship final in 1928, Cotton decided to go to the United States over the winter as part of his learning process. He went with a fade and £300 and returned with his money intact and a draw. His first important victory came in the 1930 Belgian Open and in 1933 he had his first clear chance of the Open Championship when

Henry Cotton takes part in a wartime charity match. Some of his best golfing years were lost to the war

he shared the lead after three rounds but then collapsed over the final 18 holes, with a round of 79.

He collapsed again at the same point in 1934. This time it was all right; he had scattered the field with his opening rounds of 67 and 65 – still the best start ever made in the championship. His 72 in the third round kept his momentum going and he went into the final round with a nine-stroke lead. Cotton, suffering stomach cramp no doubt brought on by his closeness to glory, played very badly for 12 holes. He then returned to form to finish a comfortable five-stroke winner. No champion had scored higher in his final round since 1911.

Cotton was always at the top of the list in the years leading up to the Second World War and the first three afterwards. Perhaps his greatest round was his fourth at Sandwich in 1938. No one got within three strokes of his 74 in a full gale. However, this didn't bring him the championship. By then he had won his second championship, at Carnoustie in 1937, which is usually considered to have been his greatest achievement because the whole of the winning US Ryder Cup team were in the field. Cotton's long game was off, but his chipping and putting were deadly.

By this time, Cotton was lording it over the British scene; he was the greatest player in the land and both looked and lived the part. He spent some time at Royal Waterloo in Belgium, where a professional's income and status were far higher than in Britain, and when he returned to Ashridge was able to demand as a precondition that the club build him a spacious pro's shop and provide facilities for his lessons. There was more money about and Cotton relished living as a man of means. Though one may think that there was little money in professional golf until recent times, the American, Walter Hagen, made a fortune and spent it. Cotton's opportunities this side of the Atlantic were more limited but he kept his money and was the biggest fish by far. He got more than a fair share in the way of endorsements, high lesson fees, journalism and he even toured the music halls. He also kept on winning tournaments and had a wealthy wife.

After the war, Cotton had to re-establish himself and largely did that with a five-stroke victory in the 1948 Open Championship when he was 41. Cotton now took the surprising decision, while still the best player in the country, not to play in the Open Championship, and also turned down a place in the 1949 Ryder Cup team. He continued to play in other tournaments. When he returned to championship golf, he was in his mid-forties and Locke and Thomson were the names on everyone's lips. Cotton showed that his long game with his long straight driving and, some declared, even longer fairway woods, and mastery of the long irons was as strong as it had ever been, but he didn't come close to winning.

Eventually, he went off to Portugal, built the Penina course and lived in the hotel. His knighthood was announced a few days after his death. The honour had been long delayed but Sir Henry had made some enemies. It is a pity that he missed enjoying the title when he was in his prime.

OPPOSITE: *In 1958 – ten years after his last Open Championship victory – Cotton was still regarded as the maestro*

BEN CRENSHAW

*Ben Daniel Crenshaw
(1952–   )
USA, was born in Austin,
Texas.
Once expected to dominate
golf, he didn't quite do that
but will go down in golf
history as one of the greatest
putters. He won the 1984
Masters.*

Ben Crenshaw came into professional golf in 1973 with a great amateur career behind him. Though never a US Amateur champion, (but a finalist in 1972), he had won the NCAA title three times in a row in the years 1971–3 and won the Western Amateur at both match and strokeplay in his final amateur season. His start in professional golf caused many to see him as the new Nicklaus: he began with a 65 in the Texas Open and went on to win by a couple of strokes. The next event was the World Open, one of those tournaments which once aimed at major championship status but faded quickly away. Crenshaw finished 2nd. His first two tournaments had brought him nearly $70,000, which sounds quite a considerable amount even today, when Tour purses have risen so much higher.

However, Crenshaw couldn't maintain that kind of pace in 1973 nor during the two seasons which followed when he didn't win anything but made a good living at around 30th on the US money list each year. In 1975 he also came close to earning his first major title. He finished just a stroke behind the play-off between Lou Graham and John Mahaffey for the US Open, beaten because his iron to the 71st, a short hole, was a little short and fell into the water.

Soon it became common knowledge that to win a major championship was Crenshaw's main ambition in life, preferably either the British or US Open. A lover of links golf, Crenshaw would probably have been happiest to win the British title. In 1976 he made what sounds like a good attempt at the Masters, finishing 2nd. However, that was the year in which Ray Floyd ran away with the event, finishing miles ahead. The following year at Turnberry, scene of that epic battle between Tom Watson and Jack Nicklaus, Crenshaw could have made it a three-horse race but fell away early in his final round. Two years later at Lytham, he was even more in the thick of it but a 6 on the 17th, a par 4, almost ensured that Ballesteros would be champion. Crenshaw finished three strokes behind in 2nd place with Jack Nicklaus, the man who had beaten him at St Andrews in 1978.

The Open Championship seemed to be the event that Crenshaw was bound to win eventually as his performances were so consistent. In 1980 he again played very well and finished 3rd – no one had a real chance against Tom Watson that year. Ben seemed to come closest to winning a major during the US PGA Championship in 1979 when he produced the remarkable scoring sequence at Oakland Hills of 69, 67, 69 and 67 for an aggregate just one above the record for the event. This was good enough for a sudden death play-off with David Graham. Crenshaw might well have won on either of the first two holes but superb putts from the Australian saved the day and Graham then went on to win on the 3rd.

Ben Crenshaw fulfilled his ambition to win a major championship in 1984 when he captured the US Masters title

However, Crenshaw got his major in the end: the 1984 Masters. He began with an almost perfect round of golf, a 67 with every green except one hit in regulation figures. When he followed with rounds of 72 and 70, he was two strokes behind Tom Kite, a man who had found winning tournaments as difficult as Crenshaw found winning the majors. The foundation of Crenshaw's win was his steady play on the first nine. He didn't drop a shot and had birdies on the 2nd, 8th and 9th. Then came a great morale booster: his second shot to the 10th was none too good and he left himself an undulating putt of perhaps 30 yards. With three-putts the likeliest result, Crenshaw holed it for a two-stroke lead. He gave one away on the next but his 2 on the treacherous 12th contrasted with 5s for Larry Nelson and Tom Kite. In the end, only Tom Watson offered a challenge with two late birdies. Even so, Crenshaw played the last knowing a 5 would be good enough to win. He got his par 4. With that major championship in the bag, Crenshaw disappeared totally for a while, ill health in the form of a hyperactive thyroid being the cause, but came back to form in the seasons 1986–8.

Crenshaw really established himself in the USA in 1976 when he won three events and was 2nd on the US money list. He also won the Irish Open on what was said to be the first occasion that he had played links golf. Since then, he has had six more finishes among the top ten money-winners and has taken 14 tournaments on the US Tour. Despite these achievements, Crenshaw has often been plagued by one weakness: relatively wild tee shots. On the other hand, many thought him the best recovery player in US golf. For many years it was a toss-up who was the better performer on the greens: Crenshaw or Watson. If imitation is a form of flattery then Crenshaw must be a popular man as his arms-only style has influenced many players.

Crenshaw's decisive singles with Eamonn Darcy in the 1987 Ryder Cup matches said quite a lot about the man's golf. He broke a putter shaft after a few holes but caught the Irishman by showing that a putter can use any club effectively – a sand iron and a 1-iron in Crenshaw's case. Yet he lost the match when a couple of wild tee shots let him down as they have done so often in his career.

LAURA DAVIES

For several years, it has been apparent that thanks to such stars as Langer, Lyle, Faldo and Ballesteros, European golf is approaching the standard of golf on the US Tour. No one for a moment, however, considered that women's golf in Europe was anywhere near the same level as that on the US LPGA Tour in America. Laura Davies therefore made enormous impact by going over to America and winning the US Open Championship in 1987. With Liselotte Neumann – another European – winning the very next year, perhaps a women's version of the Ryder Cup matches may not be far off, particularly in view of the success that the British women have enjoyed in the Curtis Cup, the match for amateurs. Yes, there certainly is a wind of change blowing through golf.

Laura had played in the US Women's Open in 1986 and did well to finish 11th. The 1987 US Open was only her fourth entry on the LPGA Tour. About four months earlier she had caused a stir at the Nabisco Dinah Shore by leading the first round with a 66 before crashing to an 83 and an eventual 33rd place finish. There was no crash at Plainview, New Jersey, however. She was all steadiness throughout with rounds

Laura Davies (1963–) England, was born in Coventry.
One of the longest women hitters ever but also has a good short game. She won the British Ladies' Open in 1986 and the US Women's Open in 1987.

Laura Davies' win in the 1987 US Women's Open made her an international star. No woman – and few men – can hit a ball further than Davies

of 72, 70, 72, 71. With a few holes to go, there was a three-way tie between Davies, Ayako Okamoto and JoAnne Carner. Perhaps JoAnne ('Big Momma') should have won but her shot to the last green was too strong and she couldn't get down in two more. A play-off over 18 holes followed the next day between Carner, Davies and Okamoto. On the 13th there was an important swing to Davies when she birdied the hole to go two ahead of Okamoto and three of Carner. The championship was virtually settled on the 15th as Laura holed a huge birdie putt to increase her lead.

Her long hitting had caused some astonishment. During the tournament, she was averaging 255 yards against 220 for the field and on one hole, measuring 493 yards, she was the only woman golfer ever to have reached the green in two. On the last play-off hole she put a ball down on the grass and played a 5-wood for safety. Even so, hers was the longest tee shot. Her 71 took the play-off by two strokes from Okamoto with Carner a stroke further away. As a result of Laura Davies' win, the LPGA changed their rules. Laura would not have to attend the qualifying school tournament and she was voted an LPGA member as the year's champion.

In 1988, her successes continued in the USA: she won the Circle K Tucson event in April and the Jamie Farr Toledo Classic in June. Laura also came close to another major, finishing 2nd in the Du Maurier Classic. In Europe in 1988 it was ironic in view of Davies' great prestige that her performances were eclipsed by Marie-Laure de Lorenzi-Taya of France, who won seven times, but Laura still managed three wins and another at the end of the season in Japan.

Laura didn't have a dominant career as an amateur, perhaps because it was a short one, but she won important events and earned Curtis Cup selection in 1984. On turning professional in 1985, she was immediately successful and topped the money list for her first two seasons.

RODGER DAVIS

Many tournament professionals over the years have tried to make themselves instantly recognisable on the golf course. Jimmy Demaret started it all off, bedecked in multi-coloured outfits, while Max Faulkner led the fashion field on British courses later on. Others were more restrained and were content to have a trademark: the Ben Hogan cap, Sam Snead's straw hat or Gary Player in an all-black ensemble which he claimed 'absorbed the heat of the sun' and made him feel stronger.

Two players, by my reckoning, lead the sartorial field in the 1980s – Payne Stewart in America and Rodger Davis on the European Tour and all points east. Both have made plus-twos their trademark with Stewart going for subtle pastel shades while Davis uses a palette of bolder colours. He also makes more of an impact by wearing socks emblazoned with his name in a diamond pattern and, incidentally, he wins more tournaments!

For a long time, Davis was overshadowed by his fellow Australian, Greg Norman, who is not far behind Davis as regards the golfing wardrobe. Davis became accustomed to finishing 2nd to Norman and to other players – in fact, he has accumulated more than 30 2nd place finishes. However, there were victories as well. In 1977 and 1978 Davis won six tournaments in Australia and tried his luck in Europe. Playing at The Belfry, he twice made a run at tournaments before turning in a round in the 80s. This proved to be a useful part of his learning experience as in 1981 he won the State Express Classic over this course, his first victory on the European Tour.

Davis also attracted attention in the 1979 Open Championship at Royal Lytham. After three rounds he was four off the lead but then reached the turn in 32. With five holes to go, he went to the top of the leader board, then, just as suddenly, a run of 6, 5, 6, from the 14th to the 16th meant he was off it again. He finished 5th, five strokes behind Seve Ballesteros.

However, Davis lost his game in the early 1980s and at one time gave up tournament golf in favour of owning and running a motel in Queensland. Unfortunately the venture failed so he started to play in Europe again. In 1985 the drought ended when he won the Victorian Open. In 1986 he won the PGA Championship at Wentworth and three titles in Australia and New Zealand, including the Australian Open. In that year he was 7th on the European money list and was 8th in 1987, when he also made another strong run in the Open Championship, at Muirfield. He began with a dazzling 64 but middle rounds of 73 and 74 put paid to his four-stroke lead. Davis came back, however, with a 69 on the last day to tie with Paul Azinger for 2nd place. Though he never quite looked like winning, he finished just a stroke behind the champion Nick Faldo.

Rodger Davis (1951–   ) Australia, was born in Sydney, New South Wales. One of the most recognisable characters in golf, he is a late developer who became an international star only after his 30th year.

A sartorial lapse by the always immaculate Rodger Davis: spot the spelling mistake

After a less successful year in Europe in 1988, Davis returned home to win the biggest first prize ever offered in Australian golf. He took away £233,000 when he won the Bicentennial Classic at Royal Melbourne, beating Fred Couples on the second hole of the sudden death play-off.

JIMMY DEMARET

Though there was a 20-year age difference between us, Jimmy Demaret was one of my favourite people in golf. He was born one of nine children of a carpenter and when he grew up as a golfer the US Tour was hardly worth playing on. You had to finish well up in a tournament to draw a cheque at all. So Demaret stayed at home in Texas where he won the state PGA Championship five years in a row, from 1934 to 1938. The winner's prize money was $25! It seems to have given Jimmy the confidence to venture out into the world of golf beyond his home state. He won his first event in 1938 and the important Los Angeles Open in 1939. In 1940, he really arrived; he won seven events, one of

James Newton Demaret (1910–84) USA, was born in Houston, Texas.
Famed for the flamboyance of his golf clothing and his elegant fade. He won the Masters in 1940, 1947 and 1950.

A pity this one isn't in colour: Demaret's trousers could be magenta, the shirt crimson with yellow stripes ...

which was the Masters. That was the year Lloyd Mangrum began with a record 64 which lasted many years. Demaret's 67 was not far behind, however, and included a 30 for the second nine. His final winning margin of four strokes set a record not bettered until 1953.

Despite a financially very successful season, Demaret was such a free spender that he had to borrow the fare home to Texas at the end of the Tour. One of the items he spent a lot of money on was clothes. Demaret wanted to be noticed on the golf course. He preferred to appear topped by a Tam O' Shanter beneath which he might well wear, say, a bright orange shirt and chartreuse slacks, with shoes made to order from matching material to complete the ensemble. It all made for good publicity; golf reporters made a point of keeping an eye out for Demaret as his clothes made good copy. What his frequent fourball partner, Ben Hogan, made of it is hard to say. His tastes went more towards matching fawns or greys.

Demaret was also usually good for a quote. Of one golf course he said, 'Man, the greens were so fast you had to hold the putter over the ball and hit it with the shadow'. Of another, 'Those fairways are so narrow you have to walk down them single file'. Later, after the first round of the San Antonio Open in 1955 when Mike Souchak had a 60 to Demaret's 74, he said, 'I don't want anyone to know I've been here. No one should come.' (Brackenridge Park was a poor public course.) A day and a 63 later Demaret was saying, 'Man, I've never seen a golf course improve so much overnight!'.

Demaret's best year was 1947: he took the Vardon Trophy for the lowest stroke average, won six events, was leading money-winner and picked up his second Masters title. In 1950, he became the first man to win the Masters three times. With six holes to play he was five strokes worse than the Australian Jim Ferrier but came through to win by two. Demaret's golf game lasted extremely well. When he was 47 in 1957 he finished just a stroke off the play-off between Dick Mayer and Cary Middlecoff and four years later was one of the pair who won the World Cup for the United States. He ended his golfing days at the Champions Golf Club which he owned with fellow tournament player Jack Burke, outside his hometown of Houston.

LEO DIEGEL

'They keep trying to give me a championship, but I won't take it.'
That was Diegel's rueful comment after yet another major had slipped
away from him, as they were to do right through his career. How
different (as with Sam Snead and Macdonald Smith), it might all have
been had he won the US Open right at the beginning of his career
when he had a clear-cut chance. Indeed, he nearly won the 1920 US
Open at Inverness. Harry Vardon had looked the likely winner with a
few holes to play but the old man's game went to pieces when a storm
suddenly blew up. Then another elder statesman, 43-year-old Ted Ray,
set a target of 295. One of the men still out on the course was Diegel,
who was three strokes better than Ray with only five holes left to play.
Par in would mean a very comfortable victory indeed. Diegel then
topped his drive at the 14th but wasn't in real trouble. A friend rushed
up to give him some information about the scoring ahead. Diegel
snapped that he wasn't interested – 'I'm playing my own game'. With
that, he hooked his second shot into a bunker and eventually took a
double bogey 6. Dropped shots followed on the next two holes and
that was that. He tied for 2nd place. 'Never mind,' they probably said,
'his time will come again. Look how young he is – barely 21.'

Diegel's chances did come again, in both the Open Championship
and the US Open, but he was never able to take them. But what a
boost to his confidence it would have been to win young, like his
contemporaries Sarazen and Jones, or Hagen, who took his first US
Open at the age of 21. Even so, Leo Diegel was a highly successful
player, despite his twanging nerves. He did win majors: the US PGA
Championship in 1928 and 1929. In 1928 he ended Hagen's stupendous
matchplay run by beating him in the third round and then crushed
Gene Sarazen by 9 and 8 before taking the final from Al Espinosa (who
tied with Bobby Jones for the 1929 US Open) by 6 and 5. The following
year, he had a decisive victory in the final against Johnny Farrell, a
brilliant putter who had won the 1928 US Open by defeating the great
Jones in a play-off. The luck seems to have run against Farrell in 1929.
With nine holes to play it was anyone's match, but Farrell twice
knocked Diegel's ball into the hole when trying to get round a stymie.
(In matchplay at the time, and for long afterwards, if your opponent's
ball lay between yours and the hole, you had to manage as best you
could – usually by chipping your ball over your opponent's.)

In the late 1920s Diegel enjoyed the best phase of his career. Tournaments came his way in a steady flow but winning the Canadian Open
was his speciality: he won it in 1924, 1925, 1928 and 1929. He never
again came as close to winning a US Open as he did in 1920, however.
Third and 4th were his best finishes.

Diegel was one of those Americans who made regular trips across

*Leo Diegel
(1899–1951)
USA, was born in Detroit,
Michigan.
Recognised as the greatest
shot-maker in the 1920s and
1930s. He won the US PGA
in 1928 and 1929.*

the Atlantic to compete in the Open Championship. After two rounds, he had a two-stroke lead on Hagen in 1929. Hagen stayed up late in the Marine Hotel, North Berwick, before the wearing 36 holes of the final day. 'Leo's been in bed a long time, Walter', someone remarked. 'Yeah,' Hagen replied, 'but he ain't sleepin'.' Diegel took 82 in the morning.

The next year he might have halted the Jones Grand Slam at Hoylake but finished 2nd, two behind Jones. His last real chance in any major championship came at St Andrews in 1933. Going into the final windy afternoon, he was tied for the lead on 216 with Abe Mitchell, Syd Easterbrook, the Australian Joe Kirkwood, and Henry Cotton. With others packing up close behind it was anyone's championship. Diegel should at least have tied the two who played off the next day, Denny Shute and Craig Wood. At the last he hit a good approach shot which left him with a putt for the championship and two for a tie. He missed the first narrowly and then, so the story goes depending on who tells it, yipped his next past the hole or played an air shot. Oh dear, 2nd again.

Diegel endlessly sought to perfect his golf and was apt to disappear for a day or two while trying to prove a new theory. One of his inventions that was all the rage for a while was called 'diegeling'. Trying to take his wrists out of the putting stroke, Leo crouched low over the ball, both elbows bent outwards. It produced an arms-only action and dazzled everyone when all his putts seemed to go down in the Ryder Cup matches at Moortown in 1929.

Perhaps we can leave the last words with Bernard Darwin who said that Diegel was 'In a way the greatest golfing genius I have seen'. Ah yes ... 'in a way'. That says it all.

OPPOSITE: *Leo demonstrates his 'diegeling' putting method – note the elbows*

GEORGE DUNCAN

*George Duncan
(1883–1964)
Scotland, was born in
Methlick, Aberdeenshire.
Renowned for his mercurial
speed about the golf course. He
won the Open Championship
in 1920.*

George Duncan was the immediate successor to the heritage of the Great Triumvirate of Harry Vardon, J.H. Taylor and James Braid. Indeed, he claimed to have modelled his own swing on Harry Vardon's though, an enthusiastic theorist, he was always making detailed changes to his playing technique.

Duncan had a remarkably long career at or near the top of British golf. He first represented Scotland in internationals in 1906 and appeared for the last time 30 years later when well into his fifties.

Well before the First World War, Duncan was recognised as a leading player and took part in big money challenge matches against members of the Triumvirate. He won the Belgian Open in 1912 and the French the following year, a victory he repeated in 1927. More important, perhaps, was his victory in the 1913 PGA Matchplay Championship, after being runner-up in 1910.

After the war Duncan was in his late thirties but still had many successful years ahead of him. The most dramatic events were to come during the Open Championships of 1920 and 1922. At Deal in 1920, Duncan began with a round of 80. As much of the scoring that day was high, Duncan wasn't out of contention by any means. However, his chances were obviously gone for the year when he added another 80 to his score on the second day. Abe Mitchell, his main rival in British golf throughout the 1920s, had started off with rounds of 74 and 73; he was 13 strokes ahead of Duncan and in command of the championship.

At about this point, Duncan had a wander around the Exhibition tent and a driver caught his eye. He liked the feel of it and paid his money. The next and final day he raced round Deal in 71 and 72. This was superlative scoring for the time over a very testing course but, even so, should not have presented Abe Mitchell with any real problems. Alas, Mitchell collapsed with an 84 in the third round and was gone. Duncan was champion by two strokes over the 52-year-old Sandy Herd.

In 1922, the championship returned to the Kent coast: Royal St George's at Sandwich. Again the scoring was high with the leading contenders averaging well over 75s for their first three rounds. Walter Hagen, out early, then made a decisive move; his 72 set a target none seemed likely to beat. And so it proved, but there was a last-minute shock in store for him.

The word spread that George Duncan, who had begun four strokes worse than Hagen, was playing the round of his life. Shot after shot settled close to the flag and, though few of the resultant putts were dropping, Duncan was having no difficulty with his pars. With the crowds long departed and telegrams already sent announcing Hagen's win, Duncan came to the last hole needing a 4 for a 68 and a tie. It was

seven o'clock. He hit a perfect tee shot and was left with his favourite shot – a spoon (3-wood) with a little cut to bring it round to the flag from the left. It looked perfect but unkindly kicked away left when it landed. Duncan chipped as fast as lightning, but a little short, and then missed the putt.

Although he won no more championships, Duncan was a leading tournament player for several more years and had an especially good record in matches against the United States. In 1921, he beat Jock Hutchison, who became Open champion shortly afterwards, and beat Walter Hagen 6 and 5 in 1926. In 1927, he recorded the only British singles win and, as Ryder Cup captain, destroyed Walter Hagen by a record 10 and 8 in 1929.

George Duncan poses in his bow tie towards the end of his great career in 1933

NICK FALDO

*Nicholas Alexander Faldo (1957–)
England, was born in Welwyn Garden City, Hertfordshire.
One of a triumvirate of British players who are riding high in the world rankings. He won the Open Championship in 1987 and the Masters in 1989.*

Nick Faldo is one of the many young players on both sides of the Atlantic who allowed himself only a short amateur career before turning professional. A youth international in 1974, he had a highly successful 1975 season in which he won four important events and the English Amateur title a few days after his 18th birthday – a record. He represented both England and Great Britain at international level.

Early in 1976 he turned professional and was soon recognised as a man of the future. The next year, he moved up to 8th on the money list and earned Ryder Cup selection, beating Tom Watson in their singles match. With this boost to his confidence, he enhanced his claim to be a top European player in 1978 when he won the PGA Championship and was 3rd on the money list. He again won this very important event in 1980 and 1981.

Particular features of Faldo's game were now becoming apparent. His swing was much admired: it produced great length with very little obvious strain. Some, however, pointed to a looping movement at the top of the backswing which might cause him trouble. Later on, much of his success was due to his superb putting. Faldo showed judgement on the greens and great confidence in being prepared to strike his short putts very firmly into the hole.

As the years passed, however, Faldo was not proving a prolific winner. From 1978 to 1982, he won only one more event to add to his collection of PGA championships. He also competed in the United States from the beginning of the 1980s because he believed that playing in better weather and on courses that were always well conditioned would help him to improve his game. At the time, the standard of competition was also much higher in the States.

1983 saw a great change in his fortunes. After playing the first part of the year in the USA with little success, he hurried over to the French Open as a late replacement – and won. Instead of returning to the USA Faldo stayed on and won the next two events as well. In that European season he won five times and headed the money list. Having neglected the US Tour to become number one in Europe, he found himself, almost at the end of the season, in danger of losing his US Tour membership. He lay 126th on the money list. Faldo returned to the United States for one event and his 2nd place tie enabled him to retain his Tour card easily.

Earlier, Faldo had enjoyed high placings in the USA but one of his prime ambitions was to win. He achieved this early in 1984 when he won the Sea Pines Heritage Classic. Other than Ballesteros, he had become the first current European player to win on the US Tour, before Bernhard Langer and Sandy Lyle.

That year Faldo played more in the USA than Europe where his

standing dropped to 12th. The following year, 1985, was far less successful in both Europe and the USA. Faldo became increasingly dissatisfied with his swing and won nothing after his 1984 Car Care Plan International. A previous Ryder Cup stalwart, he was one of captain Tony Jacklin's personal selections for the 1985 winning Ryder Cup team. Faldo lost both the matches in which he played.

In 1986 Faldo played better but the remodelled swing that he felt he needed if his game was to hold up under the pressure of a major championship was still not effective. Finally, in May 1987 he won the

Spanish Open and the confidence came back – in good time for the Open Championship at Muirfield. The spotlight, however, was not fully on Faldo because of the splendid season Ian Woosnam was having. Faldo was right up with the leaders after both the second and third rounds and he went into the last day a stroke off the lead, held by the American Paul Azinger. Faldo's final round will go into legend as he played every hole in par. It can be claimed that Azinger should have won as he was three shots ahead with nine to play but he finished 6, 5 against Faldo's par finish of 5, 4. Faldo was champion by a single stroke and his victory may prove to be worth more than Ian Woosnam's impressive total of tournament victories that same year.

In 1988 Faldo's swing, which had been changed by David Leadbetter, continued to hold up to the stress of competition. He had possibly become the world's most consistent player, and his eight 2nd place finishes during the season could certainly be taken as evidence of this. He also contended hotly in three of the four major championships. The first of these was the US Open at the Country Club which Faldo came within a last green putt of winning outright. Faldo missed only a handful of fairways throughout and in this sense played golf at the level of the legendary Ben Hogan. However, though he had gained a repeating swing, his putting was less effective. He lost the play-off 71 to 75.

Faldo went on to make an excellent defence of his Open Championship title; with a round to play he was two strokes behind the leader, Nick Price, and level with Ballesteros. Faldo's closing 71 was certainly no disgrace but Ballesteros played what he thought the round of his life and the lowest of the whole championship, a 65. Faldo was 3rd. A few weeks later he contended again for the US PGA, beginning with a 67 and scoring steadily the rest of the championship, finishing in a tie for 4th.

Despite his Open Championship victory, which in the USA earned him the reputation of being rather a dull dog because he had 'only' parred every hole in his last round, Faldo's reputation overseas lagged behind Sandy Lyle's. His tie in the US Open at The Country Club the following year did surprisingly little to improve this. Americans felt he lacked magic. His steadiness from tee to green was offset by a lack of fireworks on the greens and, in the end, Curtis Strange won convincingly. Faldo's victory in the 1989 Masters must surely change all this. Indeed, I think it has most of the ingredients to go down into golfing legend, with a charge over the final holes that not even Arnold Palmer in his heyday produced at the end of a major championship.

Faldo had been playing modest golf in early tournaments on the US Tour. Perhaps his thoughts were on the other side of the Atlantic where his wife was expecting a baby. But at Augusta, he was suddenly a different player. Perhaps he was sparked off by a putt which banged the back of the hole on the 2nd and dropped in. Thereafter he went serenely on with few errors and a rare eagle on the 13th to finish on 68, one behind leader Trevino. Though he fell away a little to a 73 the following day, few did better. Faldo found himself sharing the lead with Trevino.

In round three, Lee was gone, an 81 sending him plunging down the field. Faldo followed him. When rain halted play for the day he was three over par for the round. The next morning he completed his round weakly and a 77 seemed to put him out of contention, five strokes behind new leader Ben Crenshaw. Four putters under his arm, he departed to the practice putting green to try to choose one that would work. His attitude was still quite positive. He knew that five strokes can soon change hands – but not often.

In the final round, Faldo began to make things happen immediately. On the 1st, he raced a putt in from nearly 20 yards. Even so, despite reaching the turn in 32, there were others who looked more likely winners. He then did nothing to improve his chances by dropping a shot on the 11th for the fourth successive time. But the charge was just minutes away. He birdied both the 13th and 14th to be in with a chance but couldn't take the opportunity which the par 5 15th offers. At the 16th, however, he hit his tee shot right over the flag and then holed an impossible swinging putt. At the 17th, another went down from perhaps as much as 30 feet and struck rather too hard. On the last, he might have won outright as his birdie putt died at the holeside. At the time, however, Scott Hoch still looked the winner until he took 5 on the par 4 17th.

As others – Mike Reid, Greg Norman, Ben Crenshaw and Seve Ballesteros – cast chances to the winds, it was a sudden death play-off between Faldo and Hoch, who had a secure par all the way on the 18th. On the 10th, the first play-off hole, Faldo had to hole a missable putt for a bogey 5 and was then able to watch Scott Hoch miss from about two feet for the Masters title.

On then to the 11th, the hole that had cost Faldo dearly through the week. It was nearly dark. Faldo, with just over two hundred yards to the target, knew he had hit his 3 iron well but had to wait to see where it had finished. It was on line and, though not close, a birdie chance. He holed it. Five birdies in eight holes.

During 1988, Faldo had two more wins. The first came in the French Open in June but the climax to his year came when he won the last event of the European Tour, the Volvo Masters, at one of the stiffest examinations of golf, Valderrama in Spain. Appropriately the four best players on the Tour – Ballesteros, Lyle, Faldo and Woosnam – occupied the top four places. Faldo won by two strokes from Ballesteros. He finished in 2nd place on the European money list and 64th in the US – playing relatively little there. If Ballesteros is currently the best in Europe, Faldo is one of the three or four who lie just behind.

DOW FINSTERWALD

Dow Finsterwald
(1929–   )
USA, was born in Athens,
Ohio.
A very cautious player, he
was renowned for his shot-
making abilities. He won the
US PGA Championship in
1958.

I first met Dow in 1957 when he came to Lindrick with the US Ryder Cup team. As usual, the match seemed to be going in the Americans' favour straight from the off. I was in the first foursomes match out, partnering Bernard Hunt against Doug Ford and Finsterwald. We played well but the Americans got the putts that mattered and won 2 and 1. We ended up 3–1 down and seemed to have little chance but, over the first 18 holes of the eight singles the next day, nearly everything went our way. Even so, there was precious little margin for error.

One key match was Dow's against Christy O'Connor, all square at the lunch break. It was not a friendly encounter; Finsterwald was upset when the referee awarded the 3rd hole to O'Connor as Dow angrily pulled the ball back towards himself when he had not been conceded the putt. They played in silence afterwards. In the afternoon, Dow got his own back by claiming the hole when O'Connor picked up his own ball after putting to the lip. This, however, was about the only hole that Dow won, with O'Connor cruising to a 7 and 6 win.

At the time, Finsterwald had perhaps the highest reputation among the Americans, with many seeing him as the successor to Ben Hogan. The arrival of Arnold Palmer put a stop to all that. His bold play was in great contrast to Dow Finsterwald's strategy of hitting fairways and then going for the safest shot to the greens. Once there, he was a superb putter. He had the same approach as was favoured by Bobby Locke and Peter Thomson and he made it pay. You didn't ever see Dow with a string of bogeys on his card. Though Finsterwald was a very straight hitter from the tee, some claimed that he thought a shot banged straight at the flag was almost a failure. He liked to play the right shot and was pleased if he could fade in a high one or draw one low to the flag – if that was the ideal shot.

Finsterwald was at his best from the mid-1950s to the mid-1960s and in the years 1956–60 was in the top three of money-winners on the US Tour, coming 2nd in both 1956 and 1958. When he came to Lindrick in 1957, he had recently lost the final of the US PGA Matchplay Championship by 2 and 1 to Lionel Hebert. The following year, the event was changed to a strokeplay contest. Finsterwald did even better with this format. He began with a round of 67 to lead but really clinched matters when he went to the turn in his final round in 31. Eventually he took the championship by two strokes from Billy Casper.

Dow Finsterwald won 12 times on the US Tour and played on four Ryder Cup teams from 1957 to 1963; later, he was non-playing captain. In 1962 he tied with Arnold Palmer and Gary Player for the Masters but finished well out of the 18-hole play-off with a 77, nine strokes worse than Palmer.

OPPOSITE: *Dow Finsterwald*
on the last green in his 1958
PGA success

RAY FLOYD

Raymond Loran Floyd (1942–)
USA, was born in Fort Bragg, North Carolina. One of the great front-runners in golf history, he has enjoyed an extremely long run in tournament golf. He won the US Open in 1986, the Masters in 1976 and US PGA in 1969 and 1982.

How people change! Once upon a time he was Ray 'Pretty Boy' Floyd, manager of The Ladybirds, who claimed to be the first topless all-girl band. I'm not quite sure what to call him now. Certainly 'Pretty Boy' is long gone and Ray has become Raymond. He has been paid the compliment reserved for senior and highly respected figures in the game of being nominated to captain a US Ryder Cup team.

Floyd's Tour career started as long ago as 1963. For a short while, all was disaster – he missed the 36-hole cut in nine of his first ten events but then won the St Petersburg Open. He was still only 20, the fourth youngest after Johnny McDermott, Gene Sarazen and Horton Smith to win a US Tour event. But Floyd hardly went on to establish himself quickly at the top of American golf. Although he won again in 1965, he was never better than 24th in the money list until 1969, his first big year when he moved up to 8th and won three events, including his first PGA Championship.

No one is more respected by US professionals than Raymond Floyd: a popular choice for Ryder Cup captain in 1989

That was that for a few more years. Floyd plummeted down the money lists but revived in his early thirties. He won again in 1975 after a six year gap and then gave perhaps his greatest performance in the 1976 Masters. He began with a round of 65 to lead and then raced well ahead with a 66. His 131 was a Masters record after 36 holes and he went on to set a new mark for 54 holes with a third round 70; virtually all he had to do to win was walk round the course on the final day. He had another 70 to win by eight strokes and equal Jack Nicklaus's previous aggregate record of 271.

Suddenly, he was a major figure in the game and the Zebra putter with which Floyd had holed so many good putts at Augusta enjoyed a brief spell of popularity. Sales of 5-woods also prospered as part of Floyd's Masters strategy was based on the thought that high second shots are needed to hold the greens on the long holes. He left his 1-iron out of his bag and his high shots with the 5-wood helped him to be 13 under par for the 16 times he played the par 5s.

By this time, Floyd was a married man and credits the steadying influence of his wife for much of his success. During the 1960s, golf had taken second place to his night life, carousing with the likes of Doug Sanders and Al Besselink. Golf the following day or not, Floyd was seldom early to bed. Aided by some success in money matches (he once played a very lively one with Trevino before Lee tried tournament golf) he always made a comfortable living from the game. Burdened with the responsibilities of being a husband and father, he had to make rather more money – and did.

He went on to become one of the most successful middle-aged golfers ever, winning his second PGA title at the age of 40 and, much more remarkably, becoming the oldest player to win the US Open at the age of 44 in 1986 with a last round of 66. That, however, was not the round he considers his best. Of his 63 to start off in the 1982 PGA, Floyd says, 'Without a doubt it was the best round of golf I've ever played, anywhere in my life'. Living up to his reputation as an outstanding front-runner, Floyd went on to set record scores for the championship after 36 and 54 holes. Coming up to the last hole, he needed just a par to beat the championship four-round scoring record by two. Instead, he took a double bogey but that was still good enough for a comfortable three-stroke victory.

Floyd has piled up 21 victories on the US Tour and has won about $3½ million. His four major championship victories, when compared to, for example, one each to Curtis Strange and Nick Faldo and two to Sandy Lyle, are evidence of his stature. Floyd thought that his career would not have been complete without a US Open on his record but, though he has come close to winning it a couple of times, a British Open Championship might have been even more significant.

DAVID GRAHAM

Anthony David Graham (1946–)
Australia, was born in Windsor, New South Wales. Can claim to be the best golfer from his country between the eras of Peter Thomson and Greg Norman. He won the 1979 US PGA and the 1981 US Open.

It has often been said that there is no such thing as a natural golfer; it's just that such players as Sam Snead and Seve Ballesteros make the golf swing look natural but, like everyone else, at one stage or another they had to do their share of work. David Graham can never have felt the irritation many have felt at being called natural. Even his walk is a little stiff and his set-up to the ball reminds me of someone adjusting a machine. The head is tucked down into raised shoulders, the legs rather straight and that arched right wrist looks very calculated. Once the mechanism is ready, the swing is very measured and deliberate. It looks exactly calculated to achieve the desired results.

It's no surprise to me that David is an excellent club designer. The club is the last element in the golf swing and David will have given the matter his fullest attention.

David Graham first started to play golf at the age of 14 and he began as a left-hander for the same reason as Bob Charles: left-handed clubs were the only ones available. Unlike Bob, however, he soon changed over. By 1962, he thought he was ready to turn professional. His father didn't agree and declared that he would never speak to David again; and he really meant it. When the two met years later, what was to be a reconciliation ended in a quarrel.

Success as a tournament golfer finally arrived in 1970. Graham won twice in Australia and had other victories in Japan, Thailand and in Europe, where he won the French Open. With these and other successes behind him, Graham headed for the United States and qualified to play the Tour. He made money right from the start and won his first tournament in 1972. Though he won other events internationally, no more US Tour titles came his way until 1976 when he won twice. These successes gained him an invitation to the World Matchplay at Wentworth, a title held by Hale Irwin the two previous years. The two met in the final. Irwin did nothing wrong but was beaten because Graham holed putts from the kind of distances that cause a golf gallery to laugh as well as roar applause. The World Matchplay may not be a championship, despite its title, but it is an event which carries much prestige and has never been won by a minor player. Graham went on to better things, though his 8th place that year was the best US money list ranking he has achieved.

In 1979 he became the first Australian to win a major championship since Peter Thomson in 1965. This was the US PGA Championship at Oakland Hills. Going into the final round, he was four behind the leader, Rex Caldwell and two behind Ben Crenshaw. Graham went to the turn in 31 and then birdied both of the next two holes and, soon after, the 15th as well to seize a two-stroke lead. He needed to par in for, almost certainly, the championship and a round of 63. The 16th

OPPOSITE: *David Graham's 67 in the final round of the 1981 US Open is considered one of the most perfect rounds in golf history*

76

and 17th passed safely and he then hit a drive well right into trees but found he had a shot to the green. Then farce ensued. He overclubbed his second shot through the back though it didn't seem to matter: he only had to get his ball on the green and two-putt. He chose to play a running chip which stopped short of the putting surface. Graham's next attempt ran some five feet past the hole and he missed the putt – a double bogey 6 for a round of 65 and a sudden death play-off with Ben Crenshaw. Graham had the last laugh this time. On the 1st, he holed from 25 feet to get a half; holed from about 30 feet on the next and birdied the 3rd from 12 feet to win. Poor Ben.

There was no comedy when in 1981 he became the first Australian to win the US Open. He simply played one of the greatest final rounds in the long history of the event. His 67 wasn't just a very good score; his play from tee to green was near perfect and 33 putts is far more than a championship winner expects to take. Going into the final round, Graham was three behind George Burns and won by a shot.

Since then, he has had only one more US Tour victory, bringing his total to eight and is approaching $2 million in prize money. He has won nearly 20 times outside the USA, including the 1977 Australian Open and the Lancôme in the consecutive years 1981–2. In 1986 he was in the winning Australian Dunhill Cup team at St Andrews.

HUBERT GREEN

Golf has always been one of the more gentle sports. Few players have been physically attacked by an opponent and the worst you can expect from spectators is that, very occasionally, some may applaud your errors. Even then, this behaviour won't be directed against you personally. It's just that a few fans want some other individual or country to win. At the time, however, it all seemed a good deal more serious when a death threat was made against Hubert Green at Southern Hills in the 1977 US Open. Green had begun with a 69 to tie for the lead and followed with a 67 for the outright lead. His third round 72 kept him with the same one-stroke advantage, but a dozen players were within three strokes.

Most of these threw it away on the first nine of the final day but Green was out in 34. At this point the police began to appear around Green. A woman had phoned the FBI to say that three men with guns had been threatening to kill Hubert on the 15th green. Before he played the hole, he was given the options of withdrawing, asking for play to be suspended or he could simply continue, which is what Green decided to do. Thoughtfully, he told his caddie not to stand close to him for

Hubert Myatt Green (1946–)
USA, born in Birmingham, Alabama.
His eccentric style shows that there is more than one way to swing a golf club or putt. He won the 1977 US Open and the 1985 US PGA Championship.

Hubert Green defied a death-threat and won the US Open

the rest of the round. Nothing happened at the 15th and Green played the last needing a bogey 5 to win. He did it – just – by holing a putt of a little over three feet.

OPPOSITE: *A demonstration of the split-hands technique by a master*

After this success, many wondered whether Green could go on to become a dominant player. After all, he had been working his way up. His first win came in 1971 and others followed, but in 1974 he made a big move: with four victories he was 3rd on the money list. An even more remarkable feat came in 1976 when he had three wins in a row. The 1977 Open seemed to confirm that a coming man really had arrived.

Green had achieved all this with some very unusual features to his game. He crouches low over the ball, hands well in front of the clubhead. His fairly short swing is extremely fast, especially the hand action whipping the club through the hitting area. When putting, however, he was perhaps even more unusual. Again he crouches, this time with a leg thrown out sideways and the hands spread apart. For a time, he was an outstanding putter, but his main strength lay in chipping and wedge play.

He had another good year in 1978, winning twice on the US Tour. He should also most definitely have won the Masters. After a third round 65 he was three ahead of the field. After Gary Player's remarkable surge to a 64, however, he had to par the last three to tie, dropped a shot by three-putting the short 16th, but finished his round brilliantly by hitting his approach shot to the 18th perhaps two-and-a-half feet from the hole. His putt was always too far to the right. When he first attempted to putt, however, he had been distracted by the voice of a radio commentator close by – not helpful when you have 'this one to tie for the Masters'.

After this, Green began to slide down the money list, having never been lower than 13th in the years 1973–9. There was one later high point, however: the 1985 US PGA at Cherry Hills. He was always right in the thick of it and held a three-stroke lead on Trevino into the final round.

Green lost that lead to Trevino at the 5th but Lee immediately three-putted to allow Hubert to get level again on the 6th. He followed by holing a vital chip shot to stay level on the next hole. With nine to play, Trevino and Green were still level at 7 under but there was no real move from Lee thereafter. Green's round of 72 was good enough for a two-stroke victory and also qualified him for an automatic third Ryder Cup appearance that year. It was his 19th US Tour victory, while overseas he has won the 1975 Dunlop Phoenix in Japan and the 1977 Irish Open. He has earned more than $2\frac{1}{4}$ million on the US Tour.

RALPH GULDAHL

*Ralph Guldahl
(1912–1987)
USA, was born in Dallas,
Texas.*

*A contemporary of Hogan,
Snead and Nelson, Guldahl
reached the top before any of
them but suddenly lost his
game. He won the US Open
in 1937 and 1938 and the
Masters in 1939.*

'One shining hour is worth an age without a name.' If length of service at the top were one of the main criteria for inclusion in my 100 greatest, Ralph Guldahl would not be here. He was indeed a brief comet. Guldahl became known when he won a tournament at Phoenix in 1932 but his performance in the 1933 US Open made more noise. Going into the last round he was six strokes behind the eventual winner, the amateur Johnny Goodman. On the last green, Guldahl had a four-foot putt to tie but missed it. After that, he dropped out of sight for quite a while to return in 1936 when he finished 2nd on the money-winner's list though he had competed for only part of the season. This measure of success convinced Guldahl, who had a most unusual playing technique, that he had a swing which worked.

In the spring of 1937 came one of the most famous of Masters upsets. With seven holes to play in the final round, Guldahl looked almost home and dry until he arrived at Amen Corner. At the short 12th, his tee shot made the green but came back into Rae's Creek. That meant a 5. On the next, a shortish par 5 which most of a Masters field aim to birdie, Guldahl followed up with a 6. Although Guldahl played on well enough, the damage soon became apparent when Byron Nelson played those same two holes in 2, 3 – a swing of six strokes. Not long after, the Guldahl luck changed. Needing par on the homeward stretch to catch the leader, Sam Snead, he did rather better than catching up and won the 1937 US Open by two strokes. It caused a stir when the tousle-haired Texan paused before making his final putt to run a comb through his locks; he wanted to look right for the cameras.

In 1938, he was again 2nd in the Masters, behind Henry Picard this time, and again he won the US Open. Although he won by six strokes after a final 69, the luck was still with him. Dick Metz, who was the pace-setter, took 79 for his last round.

Guldahl's turn for the Masters lay just ahead although Sam Snead appeared to have it sewn up. He was in the clubhouse with a total of 280, a Masters record at the time. It left Guldahl having to play the last nine in 33 to win. This time, Amen Corner was no problem. He got his 3 on the 12th but then skied his drive to the 13th, leaving himself a very long and demanding second shot if he was to be on in two. Guldahl slammed a 3-wood to about six feet and holed the putt. He totalled 279, a record which stood until one of Hogan's supreme performances in 1953. Though the two men were much the same age, Guldahl's competitive career was over; his last win had come in 1940.

What had gone wrong? Perhaps it was his swing technique. Guldahl swung flat-footed and fell away onto his back foot in the hitting area. Perhaps this needn't be fatal; it's certainly not helpful. What he did with his right hand was far more strange. Guldahl had very little flexing

Guldahl shows off his swing to three US jockeys in front of the Miami Baltimore Hotel

of his right wrist on the backswing. Instead, he allowed the club to slide in his grip. I suspect his reactions couldn't cope with the task as he neared the age of 30. Guldahl claimed that he preferred the life of a club pro where he could be with his wife and family to that of a tournament player. He also said that back trouble was causing him problems and that he had achieved his ambitions anyway.

WALTER HAGEN

Walter Christian Hagen (1892–1969) USA, was born in Rochester, New York.
Outstanding in approach play and putting. He won the Open Championship in 1922, 1924, 1928 and 1929, the US Open in 1914 and 1919 and the US PGA in 1921, 1924, 1925, 1926 and 1927.

For the long shots, Walter Hagen stood to the ball with a very wide stance and then swayed back, allowing his left knee to flex far inwards as he came up on his left toe. For the downswing, most of that swaying movement was converted into a lurch but this largely happened after he had hit the ball. All this sounds most inelegant but in fact Walter Hagen's swing was saved by the fact that he always remained rhythmical and in balance throughout. However, the Hagen swing was undoubtedly far from technically perfect and must have been part of the reason for his famous wild shots. Legend has added to their number, as in the case of Seve Ballesteros, but it's likely that Hagen did hit more poor long shots than most of the great champions.

Hagen was certainly a great champion. Only Jack Nicklaus has bettered his record of 11 major professional titles and even he did not dominate the British Open and the US PGA to quite the extent that Hagen did during his best years in the 1920s. How did he do it? I have long felt that the magic ingredient in the make-up of the greatest players is their nerve. It's not the majestic power of their swings nor even very sharp putting which brings them home, but rather the ability to look at the task ahead coolly and to take a bad shot in their stride and not see it as a major disaster. Such a man is very likely to excel in the short game and Hagen certainly did. Among his contemporaries, Bobby Jones may have been a better approach putter but he could not match Hagen when it came to holing out in the six to 12 feet range. From, say, 100 yards out and closer, no one was his equal, not even Jones, who was never entirely comfortable with the short pitch.

The sand iron was invented at the beginning of the 1930s but Hagen won a reputation as a great bunker player without its help. He had to make do with a thin-bladed club and attempt to take the ball cleanly. An error of judgement could result in sand being taken before the ball, causing it to squirt forward just a few feet. Or the equally dreaded opposite, a thinned one through the green, could happen. If Hagen got a bunker recovery stone dead, it really was miraculous; the modern sand wedge merely calls for the skilful handling of an ideal club.

Walter Hagen first made a mark in the 1913 US Open – only the second tournament that he had ever played in. He came in 4th but at various points in the contest it looked as though he could win it. The achievement was little noticed as all eyes were on the young amateur, Francis Ouimet, who tied with Harry Vardon and Ted Ray and went on to win the play-off. Hagen made much more of a mark in the following year's competition. He opened up with a 68 to lead and held on to beat Chick Evans, the great amateur, by a shot. His next US Open came in 1919 and with it two legendary tales. Playing the final hole, Hagen had a putt of about eight feet to tie the leader in the

so that they were in play for long hitters. After Hogan's final round of 67, which may have been the finest round of golf ever played in a major championship, he announced, 'I'm glad I've brought this course, this monster, to its knees'. Only one other player broke 70 at Oakland Hills in any round!

The following year, 1952, was not a good one. Were age and the aftermath of his injuries getting to him? Hogan's 1953 may have been the best year a golfer ever had. Only Bobby Jones' Grand Slam of 1930 is a contender. Hogan played just five times and won five times. Two of these were the Colonial Invitational and the Pan-American Open. That leaves the four majors but Hogan no longer played the US PGA, then a matchplay event, because he felt his legs wouldn't take him round 36 holes, day after day. In the Masters, Hogan played what he considered his best four rounds ever – 70, 69, 66 and 69. He set a scoring

Perhaps Hogan's finest hour: he played in the Open Championship just once and won

record for Augusta and won by five. On to the US Open at Oakmont. Starting with a round of 67, it almost seems that the other competitors may have accepted the inevitable. Hogan led throughout and again won by five strokes.

It had long been put to Hogan that he ought to give the British Open his attention, though few Americans competed in it for many years after the Second World War. Its prestige in the United States was far lower than it had been in the days of Hagen, Jones and Sarazen. Nonetheless, Hogan listened and entered the contest. He came to Carnoustie in good time and studied the course intensively. He disliked the food, his caddie and what he thought were very slow greens, but he had come to win. Although beginning with a moderate 73 he scored lower every round. Watching his final 68, it was felt that Hogan would have gone round in 65 if it had been necessary.

Hogan believed that a man could win major championships until the age of 50, provided that he had the desire to do so. But, when Hogan was in his forties, putting changed from being a nuisance to a torment. Whether true or not, the legend grew with the years that from tee to green he remained far and away better than anyone else, but that once on the greens he froze over the ball and his putting stroke became, in the end, a stab. Sam Snead was prepared to try a different method. For Hogan, however, even the split-hands or reversed hands methods did not fit in with his conception of what a golfer should look like.

He won no more championships though he lost a play-off for the 1955 US Open to an inspired performance from the unknown Jack Fleck and only just missed a play-off the following year. As late as 1960 at Cherry Hills he was in the heat of contention until he played a pitch six inches from perfection on the 71st hole which spun back into water.

We can never establish who was the greatest player ever, but I don't know how you'd prove that anyone was a better golfer than Ben Hogan.

*Seve Ballesteros takes his
first major: the Open at
Lytham in 1979*

ABOVE: *Rodger Davis plays to the 13th during the World Matchplay in 1988*

OPPOSITE: *Nick Faldo sinks the putt that won the 1989 Masters in near darkness*

RIGHT: *Pat Bradley: a consistent and highly successful player*

LEFT: *Ben Crenshaw congratulates Sandy Lyle on his 1988 Masters victory*

RIGHT: *Laura Davies, winner of the 1987 US Womens' Open*

ABOVE: *Gary Player (left) and Arnold Palmer seen during the World Matchplay*

LEFT: *Tony Jacklin*

ABOVE:
Young Tom's last match at St Andrews in the snow. His father, arms akimbo, watches

RIGHT: *Nancy Lopez at the 1981 LPGA Championship*

Greg Norman – a fine international tournament winner

Jack Nicklaus lines one up

HALE IRWIN

'Neat' is for me the word that best describes the feel of Hale Irwin's golf game. The swing is always in control, the finish poised, and is at least one reason why Irwin has so often produced winning golf on the most difficult courses. You could say that this control was apparent from his first Tour victory: the 1971 Heritage Classic. The Harbour Town course, which was designed by Pete Dye, nearly always produces a high quality winner – in other words, not a slugger with a very hot putter but a player of style and control. As if to emphasise my point, Hale's next victory was also at Harbour Town a couple of years later.

In 1974 Irwin won the US Open. In the last 20 years or so the courses selected have always been difficult ones to play. If there's any doubt, the US Golf Association gives extra attention to the semi-rough and fringes and pace of the greens. Winged Foot in 1974 was one of the toughest tests ever put before championship golfers. No one survived it unscathed: Tom Watson, for example, was in the lead going into the final round and took 79. At the time Irwin, with scores of 73, 70 and 71 was one behind, but there were few fireworks in his final round. Irwin did have a birdie but dropped few shots in his 73. He won by two strokes and was steadier than those who started the last day in hot contention.

The players didn't find Inverness, Ohio, in 1979 easy either. This was another Irwin victory, his aggregate this time 284 compared to his Winged Foot score of 287, one of the highest in post-war US Opens. Irwin began with a 74, which put him precisely nowhere, but his following 68 equalled the day's low round and brought him up through the field. He did even better on the third day, with a 67 which contained one stroke that was a turning point of the championship. Ahead of him, Tom Weiskopf was coming on in a rush and then on the 13th, a par 5, hit a 4-iron close for an eagle. Irwin hit a 2-iron to a yard for a matching eagle to go with birdies on the two previous holes. At the end of the day, Irwin had a three-stroke lead. In the final round, though Irwin said he was choking from the 1st tee onwards, he increased his lead to six strokes by the turn. Then he found himself trying to steer his tee shots. One after another they went well off line but he was miles ahead. No one in strong contention made a move and Irwin was able to finish ingloriously – double bogey, bogey – to win by two, with his final round 75.

Irwin's consistent play has brought him much gold on the US Tour: over $3 million by the end of 1988. His best years were perhaps 1973 to 1981 when he had only two seasons out of the top seven and earned a reputation for never missing cuts. He went from early 1975 to the end of 1978 without missing any: 86 tournaments and a record bettered by only two players. Irwin has 17 wins on the US Tour, the last coming

Hale S. Irwin
(1945–)
USA, was born in Joplin, Missouri.
An extremely competent all-round player. He won the US Open in 1974 and 1979.

97

Irwin is a neat unspectacular golfer always likely to do well on difficult courses such as Winged Foot and Inverness where he won his US Open titles

in the 1985 Memorial. Unlike many Americans, he has frequently chanced his arm overseas and has won in Japan, Australia, Brazil, the Bahamas and Britain, where he became well known through his victories in the World Matchplay in 1974 and 1975. Indeed, he held on to his title until the 38th hole of the 1976 final and was only beaten by David Graham's unbelievably good putting.

TONY JACKLIN

For year after year during the 1970s, one of the main talking points in the golf club bars of the British Isles was, 'What's gone wrong with Tony Jacklin?'. Now that he has been retired from serious tournament golf for a few years, perhaps it's at last more profitable to think about what went right in his career and to evaluate his contribution to British and European professional golf. I think his contribution was enormous: Jacklin showed British players that it was possible to compete on level terms with Americans and win the great prizes of the game. Before him, players of the previous generation such as Bernard Hunt, Neil Coles and I, had little belief that we could cross the Atlantic with a chance of winning the US Open or the Masters. This also applied to run-of-the-mill events on the US Tour. We even felt like second-class citizens when it came to our own Open Championship – one of 'them' was destined to win. Would it be a Locke or Thomson year, or, a little later, Palmer, Nicklaus or Player?

Then Jacklin won the 1968 Jacksonville Open, the first time a British player had won a US Tour event since Ted Ray took the US Open of 1920. Then we had yet to learn that Americans played golf more effectively than we did. Suddenly, there was a new golfing hero in the land who became both national hero and superstar when he won the Open Championship at Lytham in 1969, the first British player to do so since Max Faulkner back in 1951. The most feared competitor, Jack Nicklaus, started poorly and was never in it. For a while, it looked as if Bob Charles might take his second Open Championship but Jacklin went into the last round with a two-stroke lead. He never lost this and finished in style with a vast straight drive up the last hole and a very comfortable par.

An even finer achievement lay some 11 months ahead at Hazeltine National in Minnesota. Many of the players hated Robert Trent Jones' course and the very strong winds of the first day. Jacklin was three under par for his first six holes and scarcely faltered for the rest of the four days. He was in the lead after every round. Again he finished in style with a long birdie putt and a win by the huge margin of seven strokes. Not long afterwards, he added to his legend in the Open Championship at St Andrews by playing his first nine holes in 29. Maybe he didn't win but Britain had a world-beater, a man who could do miracles on the golf course.

At Birkdale the following year, although Jacklin thought he was playing below peak form, he might well have won again. Then came that punch to the solar plexus of Muirfield 1972. Playing with Lee Trevino, Jacklin seemed to have stoically withstood a third round which the American finished with five birdies in a row which included two long putts, a chip-in and a thinned bunker shot which hit the flag

Tony Jacklin (1944–)
England, was born in Scunthorpe, Lincolnshire. Although never a consistent player, Jacklin was able to grasp his chances when inspired weeks arrived. He won the Open Championship in 1969 and the US Open in 1970.

Tony Jacklin heads for home during the final round of the 1969 Open when he became the first British winner since Max Faulkner in 1951

and plummeted down into the hole. With a 67 to the American's 66 he was one behind with the final 18 to play.

With two holes left to play, Jacklin had drawn level with Trevino who had to par in order to beat Jack Nicklaus, who had played almost the round of his life for a 66 which could have been at least two strokes lower. On the 17th, a par 5 just out of reach in two that day, Jacklin hit two magnificent woods just short of the green. Trevino was all over the place. Jacklin pitched up only moderately, leaving himself a putt of perhaps six yards. Trevino, through the green in four said, 'I've had it', pulled out a club, gave a quick glance towards the hole and ran it in. Regulation par. Jacklin now had to hole his putt to take the lead. Alas, he ran it too far past the hole and missed the return. 'His time will come again', said Henry Longhurst in his BBC commentary, but it didn't, you know. In the years up to his retirement, Jacklin was to win more tournaments but never again did he contend in a major championship. In a very few years, he was no more than one of the best British players and then not even that.

But Jacklin was to have a remarkable comeback. Jacklin had disliked playing on Ryder Cup teams; he felt that too much was expected of him and he didn't like being involved in failure. He also hated the unrealistic talk in the British press about Europe's chances against the Americans. And so he became captain of the European team at just the right time and gained a good deal of the credit from one narrow defeat and two emphatic victories.

Throughout his career he benefited greatly from the support of his wife Vivienne, who also 'mothered' successive Ryder Cup teams.

100

BOBBY JONES

Bobby Jones last played competitive golf nearly 60 years ago, but the details of his victories are in some ways better known than those of such modern heroes as Nicklaus, Watson and Ballesteros. The main reason for this is that Jones was always right in the centre of the spotlight, and more has been written about him than of any golfer before or since. Reporters at a championship attended by Jones didn't go there to report what happened in the general run of play. As long as Bobby was in the thick of it, they went to write about what had happened to him. One local newspaper in Atlanta, Jones' hometown, assigned a man to cover every move Jones made. He was O.B. Keeler and, with Jones' cooperation, he produced a classic golf book *Down the Fairway* which recounted the Jones story up to the end of the 1926 season.

Jones first made headlines when he was very young: he turned up at Merion at the age of $14\frac{1}{2}$ to play in the US Amateur. He got through a couple of rounds, beating a former champion and then went out to the holder. There followed what Keeler called Jones' 'Seven lean years'. These were years when he won no major championships – hardly surprising for a teenager. However, he did win the Southern Amateur Championship at the age of 15, which is not bad going.

When competitive golf resumed after the war, Jones came 2nd in the Canadian Open and then 'failed' in the US Amateur. He was beaten in the final. He also failed to win the next three years but reached two semi-finals. Jones really 'arrived' as a champion in another event, the US Open. He made the first of only 11 entries in 1920, finishing 8th; he came 5th the following year and was 2nd to Gene Sarazen by a stroke in 1922. If this reads as though Jones was working his way up, he certainly was and in 1923 he became champion. Jones wasn't satisfied with his victory, however. In his final round he finished bogey, bogey, double bogey and was in a play-off with Bobby Cruickshank. Jones said: 'I finished like a yellow dog'. In the 18-hole play-off the pair came to the last tied. Jones won by hitting a long iron over water to about seven feet.

Jones' striking rate now became phenomenal. From 1924 to 1930, he played in seven more US Amateurs, won five of them and was beaten finalist in another. He played in seven more US Open Championships: he came 2nd in 1924; lost the play-off in 1925 by a stroke; won in 1926; came a humiliating (for him) 11th in 1927; lost a play-off – again by a stroke – in 1928, and was champion in both 1929 and 1930.

In some ways, Jones' record was even more remarkable in Britain where he usually competed only if there was a Walker Cup match on. He made his first visit at the age of 19 with an American team, reached

Robert Tyre Jones jnr (1902–71) USA, was born in Atlanta, Georgia.

A legendary figure in golf, he packed more achievement into a short career than any player before or since. He won the Open Championship in 1926, 1927 and 1930, the Amateur Championship in 1930, the US Open in 1923, 1926, 1929 and 1930 and the US Amateur in 1924, 1925, 1927, 1928 and 1930.

One of Jones' greatest performances came in the 1927 Open at St Andrews: he led from the first round and won by six strokes

the fourth round in the Amateur and tore up his card in the Open. Jones was disgusted by his youthful tantrum and behaved impeccably throughout the rest of his career, whatever the provocation.

It is always said that the Amateur Championship was the one that gave Jones the most trouble, but he played in it only twice more, going out in the sixth round in 1926 and winning in 1930 – not really that troublesome after all. He was irritated by his 1926 defeat in the Amateur, however, and this made him stay on in Britain to compete in the Open Championship at Lytham. He won. Thinking a champion ought to defend his title, he came back again in 1927 to St Andrews and was in the lead from start to finish, setting a new aggregate record of 285 in the process. Jones couldn't spare the time to play in either the 1928 or 1929 Open, but in 1930 he made his last entry, at Hoylake, and became champion again.

Jones' most famous achievement as a golfer was, of course, his Grand Slam or 'Impregnable Quadrilateral' of 1930. He won every major championship that he was eligible to play: the Amateur and Open Championships of both Britain and the United States. As an amateur, he couldn't play in the US PGA and the invention of the Masters lay in the future. Jones found championship golf an immense strain and, though only 28 years old, decided he'd had enough of it. After all, he couldn't improve on the Grand Slam.

Other great players of their times have always started favourites but the attitude to Jones was very different. People speculated more about whether anyone in the field had a chance of beating him. The two other superstars of the Jones era, Hagen and Sarazen, never won a championship after 1922 when the man from Atlanta was competing alongside them. True, he was beaten on the odd occasion but no one ever beat him twice.

In the US Amateur, with matches played over 36 holes, his margins of victory were decisive. In the semi-finals and finals of 1927 and 1928, for example, they went like this: 11 and 10, 8 and 7, 13 and 12 and 10 and 9.

Against professionals, he was less successful at running away with things. He never really threw a championship away but tended to lose concentration when he had established a good lead. Nearly always, adversity brought the best from him. There was once a spell when he played a lot of golf with Tommy Armour, the reigning US Open champion. Jones used to give him strokes to make a game of it as Armour later told anyone who doubted Jones' greatness.

All these achievements came from an amateur golfer who emerged at a time when amateurs could no longer compete with professionals with any real hope of success even if they had the time and income to play as often as they liked. Jones was not from a wealthy family. For half of his playing career he was in higher education and later was in business and law. In the winter, he didn't follow the sun; he put his clubs away. In the summer, he played some of the majors but ignored all the regional amateur events in the USA and open tournaments alike. He really devoted only one summer to golf – that of 1930.

Besides his incomparable record, Jones left two other important legacies. He helped Alister Mackenzie in the design of Augusta after relishing that great architect's Cypress Point, and collaborated with Clifford Roberts in starting the invitation event at Augusta which was to become the Masters: Jones thought it would be nice to have friends from his serious competitive days along to play golf and talk about old times.

When he withdrew from competitive golf, Jones also ceased to play amateur golf and made enormous sums of money, far more, probably than the other big earner of his times, Walter Hagen. He made a series of instructional films, wrote a regular newspaper column and designed the first matched set of irons. Business opportunities poured in.

Most great players win because they are great competitors, not because they have perfect swings or even because they are superb putters. Jones, who was once said to 'try twice as hard as anyone else' also had most of the golfing talents. He was supreme with the woods and longer irons and had superb judgement of, and feel for, pace on the greens. By comparison, he was relatively weak at pitching. No one was a great bunker player until the sand iron was introduced after Jones' retirement. Hogan thought that the reason for his success was 'the strength of his mind'; this quality was something which Jones had to depend on in his later years. From 1948 he became steadily crippled year by year by a paralysing spinal disease but bore it in public with the grace he had shown through his golf career.

Roger Wethered (left) congratulates Jones after the American team wins the Walker Cup. Jones had beaten Wethered by 9 and 8 in the singles

TOM KITE

Thomas O. Kite jnr
(1949–   )
USA, was born in Austin,
Texas.
The classic example of the
player who wins more money
than tournaments, though
1989 gave clear signs of a
change.

Tom Kite was the leading money-winner on the US Tour in 1981: how many times did he win? You'd expect three or four perhaps, but no, Tom managed to accumulate his $375,000 despite winning only one contest – the Inverrary Classic. Although he had been taking part in the US Tour for nearly ten years and was a very well-known figure by then, this was only his third win. Victories have come his way more often since then and by the end of 1988 he increased his total to ten on the US Tour but has only once, in 1984, won twice in the same year. Overseas, he has not been a great winner, increasing his total by just one with the 1980 European Open at Walton Heath.

When you come to money, however, it's a very different story. Perhaps 1988 was typical. Again, no wins, but he pocketed $760,000 and came 5th on the US money list, increasing his career haul on the US Tour to well over $4 million. At the end of 1987, only Nicklaus and Watson had a better career total though Curtis Strange pushed Kite down a place with his $1 million-plus year in 1988. Of course, the constant rise in prize money makes such figures almost meaningless. Such players as Ben Hogan and Byron Nelson won only about $200,000 in their whole careers. One tournament victory can earn a player as much today and place them about 50th on the 1988 US money list. We should probably, therefore, pay attention only to *placings* on money lists, not the amounts of dollars, pounds or yen won. On this basis, Tom Kite would come virtually nowhere compared to such giants of the past as Hogan, Nelson and Snead or, more recently, Nicklaus and Watson. Apart from his year topping the money list, he was 3rd in 1982 and 5th in 1984 and 1988. Even so, forgetting the dollars again, Kite was placed worse than 9th only once in the eight years 1981–8. He must be doing something right.

Kite's great consistency was clearly seen in 1981. He played 26 events and was in the top ten in 21 of them. As further evidence of his steady play, Kite also won the Vardon Trophy, awarded for the year's lowest stroke average – 69.80. He won the trophy again in 1982, his average was 70.21 and when he missed a 36-hole cut that year, it was the first time he had failed in 53 appearances. By contrast, Jack Nicklaus never had the lowest stroke average even though he was leading money-winner eight times and piled victory on victory.

Part of the difference must be that some players respond to the scent of success. Few then produce superlative golf – that more often happens when the pressure isn't at its most extreme – but they are able to hold their games together and par their way in. Perhaps Tom lacks this spark or has become too used to making the game pay, knowing that, making it to, say, 6th place, brings in plenty of dollars.

With such a background, it should be no surprise that Tom Kite has

never won a major championship. His steady game has meant that he has many times been in contention and, for example, looked as though he might win the Open Championship in 1981 or the Masters in 1984. Sadly he didn't win either and, at the age of 40 all those best chances may be behind him.

CATHERINE LACOSTE

Catherine Lacoste (later de Prado)
(1945–)
France, was born in Paris. Although going into semi-retirement in her mid-twenties, she had already established herself in golf history. She won the British Ladies' Championship in 1969, the US Women's Open in 1967 and the US Women's Amateur in 1969.

You may have more opportunities to excel if your parents are sports stars but that situation can be daunting as well. Catherine Lacoste's father René was one of that great 'Three Musketeers' of French tennis in the 1920s and 1930s together with Henri Cochet and Jean Borotra. Among many successes, his outstanding achievement was to win the US Open Championship. Her mother was France's best female golfer

Lacoste is seen in play at Prince's in 1964

Catherine proudly shows off the US Women's Open trophy in 1967

in the 1930s and was the first overseas player to win the British Ladies', which she did in 1927. So Catherine had a lot to live up to and was determined not to be known as 'the Lacostes' daughter'. By becoming virtually the best woman player in the world, she succeeded in outdoing them.

Her finest achievement was to win the US Open in 1967 when just five days past her 22nd birthday. With a second round of 70, she went into a five-stroke lead and later increased it. With victory in sight in the final round, errors began to mar her performance but she did not fade from contention as many might have done in the face of a very partisan US crowd. She recovered her poise and came through to win by a couple of strokes. She was the youngest player to win the championship, the second overseas player, and the first and still the only amateur.

In 1969, she had perhaps an even more outstanding year, becoming only the third woman to win the British and US Amateur titles in the same year. Shortly afterwards, she announced her forthcoming marriage and retirement from international golf. She had performed so well for the French team, helping them to victory in the 1964 World Team Championship and taking the individual title in both 1964 and 1968. Thereafter, she competed little but won the Spanish title in 1972 and 1976. Earlier, she had won the French Ladies' Open Amateur title four times and the Closed Championship twice. A powerful striker, she had a rare mastery of the long irons.

BERNHARD LANGER

Bernhard Langer (1957–   ) Germany, was born at Anhausen, Bavaria. Troubled from the start of his professional career by putting, precision through the green has been an equaliser. He won the 1985 Masters.

'Once you've had 'em, you've got 'em.' This was the title of a piece Henry Longhurst wrote long ago. He meant that once an involuntary movement (the so-called twitch, yips or jerks) gets into the putting stroke, it's there for ever. The late careers of players such as Walter Hagen, Harry Vardon, Bobby Jones, Sam Snead and Ben Hogan – some of the select few who can be considered among the greatest golfers of all time – bear out what Longhurst thought. Once they began to twitch putts, they kept on doing it for ever more. In their cases the sad affliction came after great achievements; Bernhard Langer, on the other hand, was a sufferer in his teens. He was also able to prove Henry wrong. Twice he was in the grasp of the disorder but was able to overcome his problems and, amazingly, become not merely competent on the greens but one of the best putters in the world. In 1988, however, Langer had a third attack and the German maestro had to seek another cure from a condition he describes as 'like some other being has taken me over'.

I don't want to labour my point, for Langer is so much more than his putting problems but maybe club golfers among my readers are mystified about a disease that they think they do not suffer from. Perhaps you could think about it this way. What shot do you fear? Is it a drive with a cross wind pushing your slice towards the out of bounds? A tiny pitch from a tight lie over a deep bunker? A fast downhill putt? If you are truly frightened of any shot, you will probably give the shot far more attention beforehand and rehearse your swing. When the real thing comes, so will that 'involuntary movement', be it a heave or fluff. It is the club golfer's version of the professional's putting twitch.

Despite his poor putting, Langer began to emerge with some high tournament placings in 1980. Then he picked up a ladies' Acushnet Bull's Eye putter in Clive Clark's Sunningdale shop. He liked the feel of it and subsequently began to win more money. In a short time, he was the first German to win a European Tour event, the 1980 Dunlop Masters. They thought his 110 putts was probably a Tour record! For a while, Langer and his new putter were on their way. In 1981, he became the first German to win his national Open Championship and also headed the European money-winners list. He played in the World Series in the USA and finished 6th. He now knew he could compete worldwide.

In Europe in 1982, his troubles returned; his iron play was superb but one almost hoped for him that his shots would not settle too close to the hole. From, say, 12 feet, his putting was magnificent, but from five feet or less, you could bet on him to miss. So Langer simply went away, tried out a few dozen different putters and practised for hundreds

Bernhard Langer seen using a normal reverse overlap putting grip. The 1989 season was crucial for his career

of hours. He was looking for a club and a method which would enable him to feel confident. Though he continued to swap putters, he found a workable method: from long and medium range he used a 'normal' grip; from closer range he set his left hand below the right. In 1984, he topped the European money-winners list again and won four times. He also gave the US Tour an extended try.

By this time, he was always in the European limelight and was an international star – except in the United States. He remedied this in 1985, by winning the Masters and the Sea Pines Heritage Classic in two weeks. Since then, Langer has not won in America but he has won a great deal of money – over $1 million by the end of 1987.

In Europe, his appearances became spasmodic as he concentrated on the US Tour, but brilliant. When he won the PGA Championship at Wentworth and the Irish Open in 1987, his golf was some of the best ever seen. Early in the 1988 season, he came over for the Epson Matchplay at St Pierre and won. For the rest of the season, he didn't cover his expenses. The twitch had returned, but Langer worked on the problem with his usual determination and persistence. Langer tried to find a solution as his scores soared upwards. Much improved performances in the opening events on the 1989 US Tour make it seem that he may have solved his problems. As with Johnny Miller, a long-shafted putter has helped.

LAWSON LITTLE

One of the greatest golf sensations ever occurred at Pebble Beach in the 1929 US Amateur. Johnny Goodman did the impossible. After grabbing a ride on a freight train to get there, he knocked out Bobby Jones in the first round. Goodman was to win both the US Open and Amateur during the 1930s but his fame in 1929 was short-lived as Lawson Little knocked him out the same afternoon.

When Jones retired in 1930, there was much speculation as to whether a champion might one day arise worthy to be considered his equal. Surely no amateur of the future could rival Jones' achievements? But a few years later Little did so with a feat that even Jones hadn't managed: he won both the national amateur titles of the USA and of Britain in successive years. Of course, amateur golf has been much downgraded in more recent times as young players on both sides of the Atlantic rush to join the professional Tours. It wasn't so in the 1930s when the prize money for professional golfers dazzled no eyes and there were plenty of talented players for Lawson Little to beat. There are few signs of that when one looks at his results in the early rounds of the Amateur Championship at Prestwick as he won match after match over 18 holes by margins like 4 and 3. He was not stretched until the semi-final when L.G. Garnett made him play one extra hole.

It was a very different story in the final where he faced James Wallace. Little was round in the morning in an approximate 66 and played even better in the afternoon where he began with four 3s and a 4. That was all it took. They shook hands and walked into the clubhouse. Wallace had lost by 14 and 13. (By one of life's little ironies he immediately turned professional!) Little had played the 23 holes in 82 strokes; he had 12 3s; he was ten under level fours; his stroke average was 3.56 per hole. Quite possibly it was the most destructive spell of matchplay golf ever. Back in the United States, he won the Amateur Championship, beating his opponent in the final by 8 and 7.

Little, with a shut-face method, would hit an enormous draw from the tee and then select one of the half dozen or so pitching clubs he carried and loft it onto the green. Once there, he was a superb putter. All in all, he was rather like the young Jack Nicklaus who had the same game plan but wasn't allowed under the later rules to carry 26 clubs, as Little did.

At Lytham in 1935, he encountered few problems en route to the final and certain defeat was predicted for a golfing doctor from Stourbridge, William Tweddell. However, Tweddell put up some stout resistance and lost by only one hole. Little went home and completed his own version of the Grand Slam, winning both amateur titles for two years in a row. Though he came from a middle class background, Little turned professional the following year. He was

William Lawson Little (1910–68) USA, was born in Newport, Rhode Island. As an amateur, he had one of the greatest records ever but had less success as a professional. He won the Amateur Championship in 1934 and 1935, the US Amateur in 1934 and 1935 and the US Open in 1940.

Lawson Little winning the Amateur Championship for the second year in a row against Dr Tweddell at Royal Lytham in 1935

perhaps the first Tour player to be assured of comfortable beginnings because of sponsorship.

He was expected to dominate the Tour but was possibly held back because he tended to be paired with such other long hitters as Jimmy Thomson and Sam Snead. This arrangement was a spectator attraction but it hardly helped them to play par golf. However, Lawson Little did go on to be a tournament winner and reaffirmed his position in the history of golf when he won the 1940 US Open after a play-off with Gene Sarazen.

GENE LITTLER

Gene Littler was known as 'Gene the Machine' in much the same way that a writer once dubbed Bobby Jones 'the mechanical man of golf'. Both men had such good swings that hitting the ball purely seemed inevitable, though neither of them felt terribly confident. Littler even claimed that he hadn't played well since his mid-twenties when it had all felt fairly easy: you stood to the ball, swung and walked on to the middle of the fairway. As Gene Sarazen said of him, 'Here's a kid with a perfect swing like Sam Snead's – only better'. But there was a fault in the mechanism: Littler had a strong grip, and it found him out in 1957 when he began to reach the ball with a shut clubface. After a grip change, however, he was soon back on course.

Gene turned professional in 1954, just a week after accomplishing the very rare feat of winning a US Tour event (the San Diego Open)

Eugene Alex Littler (1930–   ) USA, was born in San Diego, California. Credited with having one of the simplest swings in modern golf. He won the US Amateur Championship in 1953 and the US Open in 1961.

Gene Littler, a very successful Ryder Cup player, seen at Birkdale during the 1965 match

117

as an amateur. The following year he won four times and in 1959 was 2nd in the money list, with five victories, and repeated that placing in 1962.

Though most critics commented on the Littler swing, his short game was a greater asset; he was masterly with the pitching irons and was a superb putter. His record of consistency was outstanding. In the quarter of a century between 1954 and 1979 he was only once not in the top 60 on the US money list and was ten times 9th or better. Year by year the number of tournament wins mounted up until he won his 29th and last in 1977 at the age of 47. He even kept going after an operation for cancer of the lymph glands involving the removal of muscle under the left arm in 1972 (the year in which he didn't make the top 60). He came back to have one of his very best years in 1975 at the age of 45. He won three times, was 5th on the money list and, as usual, made the US Ryder Cup team.

Gene Littler kept on making a living on the US Tour into his fifties, but by then was concentrating on the Seniors' Tour where he was an immediate and lasting success. There was, however, a flaw in his golfing make-up: Gene doesn't seem to have had the desire to be a great golfer. If he made a good start to a season, he was likely to go back to his family and collection of vintage cars (Rolls Royce being his special love). Although he won two major titles, there should have been more on his record. He did, however, come very close to the 1970 Masters, which he lost in an 18-hole play-off to Billy Casper, and he also had the 1977 PGA Championship in his pocket until his game went to pieces over the closing holes and let Lanny Wadkins in.

BOBBY LOCKE

If you were a golfer growing up in the 1930s like Locke, it wasn't unusual, if you were exceptionally good, to be given the nickname 'Bobby', after the great Bobby Jones. That's where the name came from in his case; however, he took the resemblance a stage further.

Locke had two heroes: Walter Hagen, because of his superb short game and Bobby Jones for his ease and rhythm of swing. Fittingly these were to become the key features of Bobby Locke's game. How did he measure up to his idols? Locke, though comparisons between generations can only be approximate, certainly developed a short game which was as admired as Hagen's had been in the 1920s. I have never seen a player with a better judgement of and feel for distance. Occasionally you might see him wide of the flag with a second shot but he was almost always pin high. As a chipper he was simply the best in the business and on the greens he amazed and confounded even the Americans of the late 1940s and early 1950s.

As a swinger of the club on full shots I don't believe he was comparable to Bobby Jones. Perhaps he lacked the man's lazy elegance and most certainly the whiplash in the hitting area. However, Locke learned some lessons from Jones and kept true to them. He always maintained perfect rhythm and balance and never got himself into an ugly position at any point during his swing. Early in his golfing career Locke decided that he must always swing easily so it came as a shock to him when he made his first visit to Britain late in the 1930s to find that he needed about 20 more yards from the tee. Top amateurs and professionals were hitting the ball further.

At the time, Locke played with fade. He decided not to try to change the easy pace of his swing and hit harder for more length; instead he would draw the ball. That way he would get more run. The result was just what Locke wanted. He got the length and kept the easy rhythm. However, in the mature Locke, it all certainly looked very unusual. With a wood he sent the ball way over the rough on the right from where it made a great loop back to the fairway. It was the same for shots to the green, right down to the short irons. If Locke had ever had a bad day, when the hook didn't take, he'd look a very inferior golfer indeed – just about every shot would have finished in the right rough, often miles away from the fairway. But I don't remember this ever happening.

Locke had made a name for himself by the time of the Second World War as a dominant figure in South African golf both as an amateur and later as a professional with five South African Opens to his credit. Overseas, he won three national championships – the Irish, Dutch and New Zealand Opens. The lean young man then went off to fly Liberator bombers for the South African Air Force in the Mediterranean theatre.

Arthur D'Arcy Locke (1917–87) South Africa, was born in Germiston, Transvaal. The most unathletic in appearance of all great golfers, he was gifted with a superb touch and judgement. He won the Open Championship in 1949, 1950, 1952 and 1957.

Bobby Locke drives at Stoneham in 1951 as Reg Horne waits his turn

This, too, left a mark on his quirky personality. On passenger planes after the war, he always belted his by now portly frame very firmly into his seat for the whole flight – and made sure that he was given a seat next to an exit door.

Before the war, Locke had been approaching the top of his profession and was very soon a world star on his return to golf. In Britain in 1946 he won three tournaments and finished joint second in the Open Championship; the champion was Sam Snead. Locke invited Snead to South Africa for a series of challenge matches. Snead went for the flag; Locke was content to aim for the green. He then putted the American to death, winning by 12 matches to two. This decided him to try his luck in the United States, as Walter Hagen had advised him to do many years before.

Bobby arrived in time for the Masters. US players watching him on the practice ground enjoyed the joke: the guy swung the club much too far back so it reached an absurd position at the top – crossing the line and continuing on to the right. He also had 'no left arm' and was 'flippy wristed'. Locke finished 14th and went away to win the Carolinas

PGA and the Houston Invitational. Well, he might, as they declared, duck hook every shot, but could he score! A 3rd place followed and in the next event Locke made up a seven-stroke deficit against the great Ben Hogan and won again. He won the next tournament for good measure. Locke then 'rested' with a couple of 3rd places (one of which was in the US Open) and then took the Canadian Open. He was offered the substantial appearance money of $5,000 to appear in the Tam O' Shanter event; not only did he take part, but he won the $7,000 first prize as well. He played twice more and achieved 1st and 2nd placings before going home. Locke was delighted and not just by the money; he felt that his win was a triumph for the British Empire to which he was intensely loyal.

He returned to Britain in 1949 where he won three events, and set a record which still stands with his 16-stroke victory margin in the Tam O' Shanter. In 1950, playing the same event he needed four birdies in the last five holes to tie with Lloyd Mangrum. With four long putts, he did so and then won the 18-hole play-off comfortably.

The Americans had discovered Locke's secret by this time: he hardly ever missed a fairway and he was the best putter they'd ever seen. For a while they actually banned him. Locke never forgave them for this and spent nearly all the rest of his international career in Britain, Europe and Australia. He preferred these countries anyway. In the United States, he left behind a record never bettered by an overseas-based player, thanks largely to his phenomenal 1948 season.

One of his prime ambitions had been to win the Open Championship and his first success came at Royal St George's in 1949. Harry Bradshaw managed to tie but was overwhelmed by 12 strokes in the 36-hole play-off. At Troon, the following year, Locke won again, this time setting a new championship record with 279. Two years later, at Lytham, he had his third success but Peter Thomson was ominously only a stroke behind and it was the Australian who dominated the championship for the next few years. Locke was almost a figure of the past when he took his fourth and final title at St Andrews in 1957 and equalled his own championship record and beat Thomson by three. But this was nearly the end of Locke's tournament career. Two or three years later his eyesight was damaged when a car in which he was travelling was hit by a train on a level crossing.

Locke had won over 80 events: 15 of these were on the US Tour and he was even more successful in Europe. In South Africa, in his peak years, he won just about everything he cared to enter, including the Open Championship nine times. He is the golfer I most admired in my youthful tournament days, and for my money one of the best 'pound for pound' players the world has ever seen.

NANCY LOPEZ

*Nancy Lopez
(1957–   )
USA, was born in Torrance,
California.
Caused a great upsurge of
interest in the US LPA Tour
with five wins in a row in
1978. She won the LPGA
Championship in 1978 and
1985.*

Although not the leading player every year, Nancy Lopez has been the outstanding figure on the American women's Tour since her feats of 1978. After an excellent amateur career which included places in the US Curtis Cup side and the World Team Championship, and several victories in top amateur events (but not the US Women's Amateur Championship), Nancy turned professional in 1977 in time to play a few events and achieve a 2nd place finish.

In 1978, still classed as a rookie, she set all kinds of records and won nine tournaments. She was leading money-winner, Rookie of the Year, Player of the Year and won the Vare Trophy for her low scoring average of 71.76. The five wins in a row brought about a tripling of gates on the LPGA Tour.

The following year, she was again leading money-winner and had eight tournament victories. At one point during that 1979 season she had won 17 events from her career total of 50 entries, a truly remarkable strike rate. Since then, her success rate has slowed. The arrival of a dominant new star means that the rest start to run faster in an effort to keep up. Nancy continued winning but only two or three times a season – still very good by normal standards. In 1985, however, she won five tournaments, including the LPGA Championship. She set a record by winning more than $400,000 and was again Player of the Year and Vare Trophy winner, for the third time in each case. Her stroke average of 70.73 was, and is, the all-time record. She was placed in the top ten in 21 of her 25 appearances, which displays outstanding consistency, and her run of 12 consecutive top five finishes was perhaps even more impressive.

Though her deeds brought the crowds to women's golf, her friendly, smiling, outgoing personality also had a strong appeal. Lopez perhaps does not have the desire of, say, a Jack Nicklaus to dominate the game. For instance, she allowed herself time off from golf to have two daughters. She has also suffered problems with her game, though hardly very serious ones. She has a measured, even laborious, backswing and gets her clubface into a shut position at the top. This means that her bad shots tend to be hooks. Some have pointed out that there are some ten 'faults' in her swing but she usually manages to have it all sorted out when it counts – in the hitting area. If she is off-form in her play through the green, she is apt to make up for it with her excellent putting.

After the birth of her second daughter in 1986, which meant that she played only four tournaments in the year, she became only the 11th player to qualify for the LPGA Hall of Fame when she won her 35th career tournament. By the end of 1988 she had raised this total to 39 and about 2\frac{1}{4}$ million. Surprisingly, she has yet to win the US Women's Open and has just two major championships on her record.

OPPOSITE: *Nancy Lopez has
been the leading figure in
women's golf since she burst
onto the scene in the late 1970s*

LLOYD MANGRUM

An insect may have cost Mangrum the 1950 US Open. He was in an 18-hole play-off with Ben Hogan and George Fazio for the title and was a stroke behind Hogan as he studied a putt of a couple of yards or so for his par on the 16th. He noticed an insect crawling on his ball, leaned down, marked his ball, picked it up and blew the insect off. Then he replaced his ball, holed the putt and walked off to the 17th tee. With Fazio out of contention, he could still catch Hogan; anyone could drop strokes on the tough finish of Merion.

An official of the United States Golf Association, which runs the US Open, came up to Mangrum and told him that he was penalised two strokes. Mangrum glared at him angrily for a moment and then his mistake dawned on him. The US Tour rules allowed for lifting and cleaning of balls on the green but the USGA rules in force for the championship didn't.

'Well', said Mangrum, 'I guess we'll all still eat tomorrow.' Hogan went on to win his second US Open title. Mangrum later commented that, though he knew the rules of golf, he never read the local rules in force. 'I don't know the traffic regulations in every town I get to either', he said, 'but I manage to drive through without being arrested.'

Mangrum grew up as a tournament professional in the Depression years when few players made any money on the US Tour and many wondered when they would get their next square meal. Mangrum didn't make a name for himself until 1940 when he won his first tournament, the Thomasville Open and hit the headlines with a 64 in the first round of the Masters. This score was not matched until Jack Nicklaus's third round in 1965. Mangrum couldn't maintain his pace, however, and eventually finished 2nd, four strokes behind Jimmy Demaret.

When the United States entered the Second World War in 1942, Mangrum was in the front rank of American golfers, 7th on the 1941 money list and 4th in 1942. During the war Mangrum served under General Patton in the invasion of Europe and was twice wounded during the battle of the Bulge. Very fittingly for a golfer, he was sent to St Andrews to recuperate and won the GI Championship over the Old Course while he was there.

He was in the top ten money-winners for the nine years beginning in 1946 and started to carve a place in golf history by winning the US Open in the first post-war event. Ben Hogan was again involved. Mangrum came to the last hole at Canterbury, Ohio, needing a par 4 to tie. His second shot finished five or six yards from the hole but Hogan then took three putts. But it wasn't all over for Mangrum. He found himself tied with Vic Ghezzi and Byron Nelson, who should have won it but dropped two shots on the last three holes.

Lloyd Eugene Mangrum (1914–73)
USA, was born in Trenton, Texas.
A leading figure in US golf for several years after the Second World War. He won the 1946 US Open.

Out they went the next morning to play off over 18 holes and were out again in the afternoon after all three had been round in 72. Ghezzi and Nelson soon left Mangrum trailing but he then began holing some putts while the other two made mistakes. With a hole to play, Mangrum led Nelson by two strokes and Ghezzi by one. In pouring rain with lightning flashing overhead he hooked his tee shot and confronted the problem of drawing his shot to the green around a tree. The hook didn't take and Mangrum was bunkered and took three more to hole out. That was good enough. Ghezzi missed a short putt for his par and a tie.

It had been a long struggle and Mangrum was to be involved in another great struggle three years later. In a play-off with Cary Middle-coff for the Motor City Open the two agreed to call it a tie in the gathering dark after they had halved 11 holes in a row, to create a US Tour record.

Though the 1946 US Open was Mangrum's only major championship, he had three more top four finishes in the US Open and was only once out of the top six in the US Masters in the period 1948–56. His greatest achievements, however, were on the US Tour. His best year was 1948 with eight wins (only Nelson, Hogan and Snead have won more in a single year) and he won four or five in a season several more times. By the end of his career, he had amassed 34 US Tour victories and 46 victories in all. He was leading money-winner in 1951 and took the Vardon Trophy for the best stroke average in 1951 and 1953.

Mangrum was no power player and attracted very little attention for his long game, but he was a superb chipper and putter. With his centre-parted hair, moustache and ever-present cigarette he was highly recognisable but perhaps looked more like a riverboat gambler than a professional golfer. He was one of the great characters of my early career.

OPPOSITE: *Lloyd Mangrum at Wentworth in 1953 where he captained the winning US Ryder Cup team*

GRAHAM MARSH

*Graham Marsh
(1944–   )
Australia, was born in
Kalgoorlie, Western
Australia.
One of his country's most
successful international
players over the last 20 years.*

Graham Marsh is the kind of professional golfer that I sometimes think I admire the most: he is not a power hitter and is no great wizard on the greens. He just gets on quietly (in great contrast to his brother Rodney, the former Australian Test wicket-keeper), doing his job with maximum efficiency and minimum drama. All this has brought him more than 30 victories worldwide. Strangely, perhaps, Japan has seen more of his successes than anywhere else.

Graham Marsh was a maths teacher when he was runner-up for the 1967 Australian Amateur and won his own state title in Western Australia. With a job to fall back on if he failed, he decided to try professional golf. In 1970, he won a tournament in New Zealand. Marsh then pondered trying his luck in Europe; he did so and won his very first event – the Swiss Open. He was quickly just as effective on the Asia Circuit, where he was number one money-winner in 1972 and 1973. He also began winning in Japan from 1972 onwards and his record there is phenomenal, with more than 20 victories between that first one and the 1987 Taiheiyo Pacific Masters. His best year in that country was probably 1974 when he won four times, but he also had three wins in both 1976 and 1977.

The latter was perhaps his best year in international golf. In the United States he won the Heritage Classic and took the Lancôme and the World Matchplay in Europe. But for Watson's great year in winning both the Masters and Open Championship, Marsh could have claimed to be player of the year internationally. As it was, he stood 3rd on the world money list.

Oddly Graham had, at that time, achieved little in Australia. He didn't win anything until 1976, when he won his home state Open title, but he has done rather better since then, winning three events in 1982 and one in 1983. Alas, none of these was the Australian Open though he has taken his country's PGA title and the Australian Masters. The major titles are the ones missing from Marsh's record and their absence prevents Marsh from being considered one of the handful of greatest players of the last 20 years.

He did get quite close to winning the Open Championship at Birkdale in 1983. He was out early on the last day, eight strokes behind the leader, Tom Watson. At one point near the end of his round he was the championship leader, on paper, and eventually with seven birdies and no bogeys he was home with a 64. As the wind freshened it looked possible for a while that his 277 total might be just good enough for a tie at least. But it wasn't to be, and Marsh finished in 4th place, a couple of strokes behind champion Tom Watson.

OPPOSITE: *Graham Marsh
recovers from sand during the
1977 World Matchplay
which he won*

CARY MIDDLECOFF

Cary Middlecoff
(1921–   )
USA, was born in Halls,
Tennessee.
A leading US Tour player in
the 1950s. He won the US
Open in 1949 and 1956 and
the 1955 Masters.

They say it was Tommy Armour who first demonstrated just how slowly tournament golf could be played. Years later, Bobby Locke was much criticised in Britain for slow play; in private he admitted he had learned to play at his measured pace in the United States. Perhaps he'd been watching Cary Middlecoff who is reputed to be the slowest of them all – though plenty would beat him today.

An intense thinker about the game, Cary believed that getting set up correctly was vital – this is commonplace today, but 30 years ago the importance of alignment with the target was not universally recognised. It all took Cary quite a long time. He was 'slow' in another quite different way: his swing was highly unusual in that he stopped at the top quite perceptibly. In theory this can seem a good idea as it certainly should mean a player doesn't begin the downswing in too much of a rush. In practice, however, it normally destroys rhythm, but Middlecoff made it work for him. (Oddly, when he gave up tournament golf the pause, he said, 'just went away'.)

While qualifying as a dentist, Cary made a habit of winning the Tennessee Amateur title. He had also won the 1945 North and South Open as an amateur. After US Army service his thoughts turned to professional golf. He was invited to play in the 1947 US Walker Cup team but declined: as he was considering turning professional, he didn't think it right to play. Such meticulousness is not the fashion nowadays! Middlecoff won on Tour that year but really became a name to reckon with when he won the US Open in 1949. He began at Medinah with a 75 but then put together rounds of 67 and 69. His lead into the final round was by three on Clayton Heafner and six on Sam Snead. Wracked by nerves, Middlecoff could do no better than 75 but both Snead and Heafner, needing par to tie on the last few holes, couldn't quite do it.

Nobody had much of a chance to win the Open for the next few years after Hogan made his triumphant comeback, but Middlecoff won again in 1956. Despite a couple of 7s, he began with rounds of 71 and 70 to be two strokes behind Peter Thomson and one behind Hogan. His 70 on the morning of the final day gave him the lead. In the afternoon he played a very steady first nine and a run of birdies afterwards meant that he needed 'only' to par the last three holes to set a target that surely no one could match. He dropped shots on both the 16th and 17th and followed with a poor drive at the last and could not reach the green from the rough. However, his pitch was a beauty, stopping a couple of feet from the hole. His second 70 of the day was just good enough. Neither Julius Boros nor Ben Hogan could quite manage to tie.

Middlecoff played a remarkable US Open the very next year. He began with rounds of 71 and 75 to be eight strokes behind the lead. He

Cary Middlecoff was the
leading US Tour player in
the 1950s

followed with a 68 to make up a good deal of ground, but the final afternoon he came to the last four holes needing to birdie two of them to tie. He got one of them on the 16th and the other on the last, holing from about ten feet. It was one of the great finishes of US Open history and his second 68 of the day. For the 18-hole play-off the next day, Dick Mayer appeared with a camping stool, his own comment on Middlecoff's slow play. If it was a psychological ploy, it certainly worked. He shot 72, Middlecoff 79.

Middlecoff's remaining major was the 1955 Masters. He made his move with a 65 in the second round and went on to win by what was then the record margin of seven strokes. The 2nd place man, Ben Hogan, only once equalled Middlecoff's scoring in any one round.

Despite his three majors, Middlecoff had an even better record as a US Tour player. His 37 wins place him 7th on the all-time list. He was 2nd on the money list four times – 1949, 1951, 1952 and 1955. In both 1949 and 1955 he won six times. His last win came in 1961, when he was 40 years old. He retired soon after, mainly as a result of back trouble. In retirement, Middlecoff did more thinking about the game. His book, *The Golf Swing,* is writing on a par with Bobby Jones', the best writer on the game who was also a great player.

OPPOSITE: *Cary gets off to a hot start in 1949*

JOHNNY MILLER

'Happiness is knowing even your worst shot will still be quite good.' So said Johnny Miller in the days, some 15 years ago, when the drives were flying long and straight, the irons rifling in at the flag and lots of putts were dropping. That was around the years 1973 to 1976, and 1974 in particular. That year, Miller was leading money-winner and won eight tournaments on the US Tour – an incredible feat considering that accumulating four or five wins today is thought almost superhuman. He opened that magical season by winning the Crosby and followed up with the next two at Phoenix and Tucson. He 'failed' next time out but brought his sequence of par or better rounds to 23. By the end of April he had played in 11 events and won five of them but instead of making the most of it, Miller began to play a lot less. He went off the Tour for a couple of months. One reason, he said, was that he always became bored with golf by about Masters time and needed to make a fast start to his season to earn a good living. But 1974 was rather different: he won again at Westchester, just before the US Open and twice more in September before bringing his total for the year to nine with a victory in Japan.

He certainly got that fast start again in 1975. At Phoenix his scores were 67, 61, 68, 64. The man in 2nd place was a small matter of 14 strokes behind. Only Bobby Locke had finished further ahead in a US event.

Time for Tucson again. Miller played brilliantly throughout and sharpened his game even more in the final round. The result? A 61 and a nine-stroke victory. A little later came the Masters. Perhaps boredom was setting in. He did nothing for the first two rounds and was ten strokes off the lead. Then came the best final 36 holes ever in this major championship – a 65 and a 66. Though the title went to Nicklaus, with Miller and Weiskopf a stroke behind in 2nd place, it was a glorious charge.

In 1976, Miller kept up his early season habit with wins in Tucson and the Bob Hope Desert Classic. Although 'late' in Miller's personal season, he had already proved he could play in July in the British Open. He was 2nd in 1973 and 3rd in 1975 and came to Birkdale in 1976 keen to add to his major championship tally which, standing then at one, did not compare well with his winning flair in ordinary tournament golf.

The very youthful Seve Ballesteros took all the early headlines but Miller was in contact going into the final round. First he made up the two-stroke deficit and by the time he reached the 9th tee was three ahead. Miller settled it on the 11th, 12th and 13th. First he had a par 4 to the Spaniard's 7 and then followed with a birdie and a chip-in for an eagle. The rest of the way he had little to do except encourage Seve

John Laurence Miller (1947–   ) USA, was born in San Francisco, California. For a couple of years or so he played golf of a quality never bettered. He won the Open Championship in 1976 and the US Open in 1973.

not to forget about 2nd place. Miller finished with a 66 and a six–stroke victory margin. He was at a new peak in his career for this championship victory had entitled him to a place in a tournament among the greats. Let's go back in time to see how Miller made his earlier moves to the top.

It all began back in 1964 when he took the US Junior Championship. A couple of years later he proved to himself that he could compete with the best when he went to the Olympic Club in San Francisco thinking he would caddie in that year's US Open. Instead he qualified to play and finished 8th, the leading amateur. In 1969 he turned professional and moved steadily up the money list during his first four years, winning twice. In 1973 in the US Open at Oakmont, he was unnoticed as he went out to play his final round. He had begun steadily enough with rounds of 71 and 69 but then had a 76. He was six strokes behind the leaders. He began with four straight birdies and was suddenly in contention. Miller dropped just one shot in the rest of his round and made five more birdies. He came in with a 63 and no one proved able to match his total of 279. That 63 is still the lowest final round in a major and was not equalled in any round of the US Open until 1980.

Although Miller didn't win again on the US Tour that year, he did go on to take individual honours in the World Cup. He was also established as a star – perhaps a great one.

By the time of his Birkdale victory he had won 17 events on the US Tour but in 1976 was down to 14th on the US money list after 1st and 2nd finishes. In 1977 he dropped to 48th and in 1978 was 111th. What went wrong? Miller probably didn't know himself. He gave two very different explanations. Perhaps, he thought, he'd done too much manual work on his ranch to the detriment of his golf swing. On the other hand, he'd reached the top. It was being said that he was the best player in the world. Perhaps Miller didn't have the force of will to stay there. After all, he was very comfortable financially with endorsement contracts flowing in which guaranteed him many thousands of dollars every year.

After July 1976 he was never the same man. True he did make a comeback of sorts. At the end of 1979 he was much relieved to win the Lancôme in Paris and in later years he was to win again in the US – six events in the years 1980–7 and in 1981 he also took the $1 Million Sun City Challenge in southern Africa. Even so, the true magic never returned and in 1988 Miller was 169th on the US money list.

OPPOSITE: *Johnny Miller in action*

OLD TOM MORRIS

*Thomas Morris
(1821–1908)
Scotland, was born in
St Andrews, Fife.
For some 20 years he was one
of the world's two best golfers.
He won the Open
Championship in 1861,
1862, 1864 and 1867.*

The deeds of the elder Morris have been obscured by the undoubtedly superior brilliance of his son but, none-the-less, Old Tom became a figure for veneration, a Grand Old Man, in an age when so many died young.

He began playing golf at St Andrews at the age of six or earlier and as a young man his game was brought on by playing with Allan Robertson, to whom he became apprenticed as a feathery ball and club maker. Allan was his partner in some of the famous challenge matches of the day which were played for side stakes of as much as £200, then

Old Tom Morris, here seen late in life, was Open champion four times. Note his strong right-hand grip and weak left

a vast sum and far more than was ever put up for tournaments for many years.

After a quarrel between the two men, Tom Morris set up as a ball-maker and then in 1851 went off to be professional to the new Prestwick Golf Club. He was still there in 1860 when the first Open Championship took place over the club's 12-hole course. Tom was 39 and the favourite but came in 2nd to Willie Park. The history of the early years of the Open Championship is bound up with Park and Morris who dominated the winning position until the arrival of Young Tom Morris.

Tom Morris was more successful than Willie Park and remains, because of his 1867 victory, the oldest winner of the championship. He continued to compete in the event for very many years and was still a possible winner when in his early sixties. One fault, however, he had both early and late in his career was short putting. This was so bad that a postcard, jokingly addressed to 'The misser of short putts' when he was at Prestwick came, as intended, through his letter box. When considering his record, however, it is worth remembering that he would inevitably have won more titles had the powers that be 'invented' the Open Championship while Tom Morris was a young man. But matchplay was the thing and Tom Morris was very likely the best player right through the 1850s.

In later life, he was greatly in demand for laying out courses and is credited with creating many of the great courses of the British Isles, much though they may later have been changed. You could call him the first golf architect.

YOUNG TOM MORRIS

Tommy Morris
(1851–75)
Scotland, was born in
St Andrews, Fife.
The undisputed genius of the
age. He won the Open
Championship in 1868,
1869, 1870 and 1872.

When we see faded pictures of old gentlemen in long beards, most unsuitably dressed for performing the golf swing, perhaps most of us feel that these golfers could hardly have competed with the Vardons, Hagens and Nicklauses of later years. We are probably wrong and may forget that we are seeing these gentlemen portrayed in their later years, just as we can occasionally see the Sarazens and Nelsons today. There isn't the same problem with Young Tommy Morris, the wonder of his times, because the poor man died before he had time to accumulate much in the way of whiskers. Even so, he was supreme among the players of his day in a way that no one has quite managed to surpass in the century and more since his death. Davie Strath was his closest rival but he only once managed to run Tom close in an Open Championship. In 1872, he led Young Tommy by five strokes going into the final round of 12 holes at Prestwick, yet lost by three.

Not long after Young Tom's birth, his father moved to Prestwick to keep the green there. His son learned golf at Prestwick and emerged as a formidable player soon after they returned to St Andrews. He turned professional at the age of 16 and immediately beat a full professional field in a tournament at Carnoustie and followed this up by defeating Willie Park, Open champion the previous year, 1866, in a challenge match. Young Tom had played in that Open, aged 15, and finished 9th. In 1867 he was 4th – five strokes behind his father. There was no stopping him thereafter. Aged 17, he was Open champion by five strokes and repeated the feat the following year. His closest rival, Bob Kirk, was 11 strokes behind.

When the Earl of Eglinton had presented the original trophy, a splendid morocco belt, he had never imagined that anyone would win the thing outright with three consecutive wins but Young Tommy did so in 1870. This time, the 2nd place men were 12 strokes behind and no one before or afterwards matched Tom's total of 149 for three rounds of Prestwick's 12 holes. The best single round any other competitor managed was a 52 (Willie Park had rounds of 55, 59 and 60 when he won the first Open Championship at Prestwick in 1860). Young Tom was round in 47, 51 and 51. His margins of victory are worth emphasising for it must be more unlikely to win by ten or a dozen strokes over 36 holes of golf than over 72.

The Open Championship now came to a halt. Young Tom had won the belt outright. There being no trophy available in 1871, there was no championship either. If you ever get a chance to examine the hallmark on the present claret jug, you will find that it was made in 1873. However, Prestwick, St Andrews and the Honourable Company of Edinburgh Golfers playing at Musselburgh had decided to present the jug in 1872. Sensibly, they made the proviso that no one should ever

Young Tom Morris wears the first Open Championship trophy – the Belt. He was allowed to keep it after winning the event three times in a row. Nowadays no one can keep the claret jug, no matter how often they win

be able to win it outright but that he should have a medal to keep and a small money prize.

In 1872, Tom won again – his fourth victory in a row. Legend has it that he then promptly died but this was by no means so. For his final three years, Young Tom ceased to dominate the game. Possibly his example had shown others that they needed to raise their standards of play in order to compete with him. This was to happen again 20 years later, when first J.H. Taylor and then Harry Vardon changed people's conceptions of how well it was possible to play golf.

In the first Open to be played at St Andrews, Young Tom came 3rd and in 1874 he came 2nd. In 1875, as far as I can find out, neither Tom Morris Junior nor Senior competed at Prestwick. The event was sometimes arranged quite hurriedly so perhaps they didn't hear about it in time!

On Christmas Day, 1875, Old Tom called his son down for breakfast but there was no reply. Young Tom was dead, the result, so an autopsy showed, of a ruptured artery under the right lung. He had made no sound.

No photographs have come down to us of Young Tom playing golf, just a painting, a photograph and a tomb stone all showing him addressing the ball. Contemporaries all agreed, to quote one, that he was 'the best player who ever addressed himself to a ball'. Probably he had a fast swing and he certainly hit hard, perhaps harder than players before him did. He also raised standards in the short game, being arguably the first player to try to put stop on the ball when approaching with irons. He was also, despite the rough greens of the time, an outstanding putter. He was deadly from short range and was always looking to hole putts of any length.

Had he lived, we can speculate that Young Tom would have recovered from the fall from the highest playing standards which he suffered in his early twenties. The kind of golf we play does change with the years, and Morris might have gone on to win ten or a dozen Open Championships.

(*Note*: Young Tom Morris's scores are given wrongly for the years 1868 and 1869 in both the *Golfer's Handbook* and *The Royal and Ancient Championship Records, 1860–1980.*)

KEL NAGLE

Many players have just one chance at a major championship and fluff it. If they are young, it's often said: 'His chance will come again'. But often it doesn't.

Kel Nagle had few clear-cut chances of a major, but took the 1960 Open Championship at St Andrews magnificently. He began with rounds of 69 and 67, which ought to have been good enough to lead. The Argentine Roberto de Vicenzo, however, had made one of the best starts ever with two rounds of 67. In the third round he gave ground with a 75 while Nagle held on with a 71. This gave him a lead into the last round of two on de Vicenzo with Syd Scott and the menacing figure of Arnold Palmer four behind. Nagle had started a 35–1 outsider but enjoyed the support of his fellow Australian Peter Thomson. Peter had a bet on Nagle and had encouraged him to compete outside Australia.

The battle throughout that final round was one of contrasts, the dashing Palmer in pursuit of Nagle, a steady player who kept the ball in play and putted brilliantly. Palmer began as though he were after a 65, by pitching dead at the first two holes but Nagle had birdies of his own and after nine holes retained his four-stroke lead. Palmer made up some ground in the second nine, however. The gap was only two strokes as he played the 18th, which he birdied. As Palmer holed the putt, Nagle was on the 17th green. When the roar came back to him, he knew he mustn't miss his par putt from about seven feet. Nagle got it. There was never any doubt about his par to win on the last. He drove straight, pitched well and putted up close. He won by one stroke, at the age of 39.

Nagle was a late developer who drastically changed his game during his career. At one period he disappeared from the golf scene when he was a long but wild hitter and poor putter. When he turned up again, the Nagle of St Andrews had been moulded: no great length but straight and on the greens he seemed to have a magic wand. We saw the best of Kel Nagle in his forties. He gave several excellent performances in the Open Championship and was the only man to threaten Palmer during his dazzling display at Troon in 1962. At one point Nagle caught him and though he finished six behind, he was still five better than anyone else in the field.

In 1965 he had a chance of winning the US Open and made the best of it. With three holes to play, Gary Player held a lead of three strokes. He suddenly dropped two strokes at the 16th, a par 3, while Nagle was getting a birdie at the 17th. In a matter of seconds the pair were level and so they finished. The 18-hole play-off, however, quickly went Player's way. He was five strokes up after eight holes, partly a result of Nagle being upset when a wild shot into the crowd hit a spectator

Kelvin David George Nagle (1920–)
Australia, was born in Sydney, New South Wales. One of the few players who genuinely enjoy the stress of competition, he was good at taking his chances. He won the Open Championship in 1960.

*Kel Nagle won the centenary
Open at St Andrews in 1960*

and cut her badly. Nagle was unsettled and never threatened Player the rest of the way.

Nagle had more than 20 victories in Australia, ten in Europe and he also won the Canadian Open. He went on to be a great success as a Senior golfer. He won the British title in 1971 (including a round of 62) and defeated Julius Boros for the world event. He nearly won both again in 1973 (but was beaten on the 41st by Sam Snead), but managed it in 1975. The mature Kel Nagle is one of the best examples of how steady play, with few dramatic effects, can often work out for the best.

TOMMY NAKAJIMA

The prize money that can be earned on the Japanese Tour means that most of their players are reluctant to make anything approaching a sustained assault elsewhere. Their overseas appearances often happen solely because a Japanese firm is sponsoring a tournament in, say, the United States or Europe. Suntory, Epson, Canon or Honda, for example, want a Japanese face to increase television coverage back home and a Japanese player or two accepts the appearance money on offer and takes part. Tommy Nakajima, however, is the exception. He intends, though perhaps not passionately, to make himself an international reputation. He often appears in the Open Championship or the World Matchplay and has also played many tournaments in the United States.

His efforts have not been rewarded with a tournament victory, but his considerable experience makes him the most likely current Japanese player to win a major championship. Some of those experiences, alas, were daunting indeed. In the 1978 Masters Nakajima began with a round of 80 and was trying to make up ground on the second day. An

Tsuneyuki Nakajima (1954–)
Japan, was born in Gumma. A leading player on the Japan Tour through the 1980s.

Tommy Nakajima has had his share of disasters, but is nonetheless a very successful player

145

eagle at the 485-yard 13th, he reckoned, would help the cause. He hit his drive a touch too far left, caught the trees and his ball fell into the creek. He dropped out under penalty and knocked his next up the fairway safely. He then pitched his fourth into the creek which winds across the front of the green. However, Nakajima thought it was playable – and so it was. His ball rose almost vertically and came down on his shoe: penalty two strokes. He then touched the water for another two-stroke penalty (grounding a club in a hazard). Four strokes later he had got his 13 but it would have been a good deal better without those five penalty shots.

Some three months later Nakajima was at the Open Championship at St Andrews. There were no 80s this time. He began with rounds of 70 and 71 and came to the 17th, the Road Hole needing two par 4s for another 71 and a good chance for the championship the next day. His second reached the front of the green and from there his long putt curled away into the Road Bunker. He got it out with his fourth attempt. Some now call that Road Bunker 'the Sands of Nakajima'.

Nakajima turned professional in 1975, a couple of years after winning the Japan Amateur Championship. In 1977 he won the Japan PGA Championship and did so again in both 1983 and 1984. In 1985 and 1986 he won the country's Open Championship and was leading money-winner in 1982, 1983, 1985 and 1986. His best year was 1983 when he won nine events and he did nearly as well in 1986 with seven victories.

The happenings at the Masters and the Open Championship in 1978 have meant that we writers and commentators keep an eye open to see what should befall Tsuneyuki, but in general he has suffered only the normal share of misfortunes. In 1986, however, he went into the final round of the Open Championship at Turnberry in 2nd place, a stroke behind Greg Norman. He promptly three-putted the 1st from five feet to allow Norman a three-stroke lead. On the 3rd, he took a 5 while Norman holed a bunker shot from 40 yards. That was virtually that; Nakajima had a 77 to finish nine behind the Australian in 8th place.

Later in the year, he played some of the most brilliant golf yet seen in the World Matchplay at Wentworth. Alas for Tsuneyuki, Sandy Lyle did that vital bit better, winning on the 38th green in their second round match.

The President of the Immortals seems not to have quite finished with Nakajima. Playing in the 1987 US Open at the Olympic Club in San Francisco, he was tied for the second round lead and was still in contention with three to play on the third day. Nakajima finished bogey, bogey, double bogey. His main problem on one of the holes was that his ball obstinately remained stuck in a tree. However, all has not been gloom and woe for Nakajima. All those successes in Japan have made his fortune and he has won some $400,000 in the US as well.

BYRON NELSON

When Bobby Jones retired in 1930 at the age of 28, he must have been aware that he had done enough to be rated among the greatest golfers of all time. There were no more worlds left to conquer. Byron Nelson also retired at his peak, when aged 34. In his case, there was something left to prove, a few questions unanswered. His total of major championships, for example, leaves him well behind quite a few great figures in the game. It could not have seemed so to Nelson himself, however; after all, his dominance of American golf had been total.

Let's see how it went. In 1944, tournament golf was resumed and Nelson had a very good year. He won seven times and set a new stroke average record of 69.67, but he wasn't satisfied. He felt that he ought to be able to save a stroke per round. That would mean more wins. He went through the notes he kept to see where he might make improvements. Of course, there was always the putting. Nelson felt that he'd have to live with his reasonable talents on the greens and could hardly hope to improve on the consistency of his ball striking. But the notes did reveal one extremely simple truth, that he threw away the odd shot when his mind wandered. He must see that it didn't.

*John Byron Nelson (1912–)
USA, was born in Fort Worth, Texas.
His phenomenal run of tournament successes in 1944 and 1945 has never been approached. He won the US Open in 1939, the Masters in 1937 and 1942 and the US PGA in 1940 and 1945.*

Byron Nelson pictured just before he reached the top

Byron Nelson, surrounded by members of the American team, accepts the Ryder Cup from the prime minister, Harold Wilson

In 1945, Nelson knocked a stroke and a half a round off his 1944 figure. It helped him produce easily the greatest winning streak of all time. From 11 March to 4 August he won every event he entered – 11 wins in a row. No one before, or since, has bettered four. Then he lost. Undeterred, Nelson won another seven official events and another which doesn't count on his record because the prize money wasn't high enough. Through that miraculous season, Nelson played 120 rounds at a stroke average of 68.33 and was 320 under par. In one spell, he played 19 consecutive rounds under 70. In one tournament, in Seattle, he tied the PGA record with a 62 and also the four round record with 259.

Today, these feats seem impossible and as a result people have sought reasons to downgrade Nelson's achievement. They say that some of his best contemporaries were away in the armed services; that the courses were easier because the rough was cut down to save lost balls; and that preferred lies were often allowed because of poor conditioning. Though what was said about golf courses was sometimes true, the rest of these arguments ignore the fact that Byron Nelson was already long established as one of the very best American golfers, with Hogan and Snead. I'd like to examine that record.

Byron Nelson came into golf via the caddie route at the age of 12 and, untaught, was soon able to break 80. Then steel shafts came in and because of their different characteristics, compared to hickory, Nelson found himself with a vast hook. To combat it, he developed a striking method which went against the age-old thought of 'hitting against the left side'. Instead, Byron allowed himself lateral body movement through the hitting area, kept his hands ahead of the ball and drove through very low. It has been called 'the birth of the modern method'. It made Nelson an extremely straight hitter, one of the very few great players who did not favour either a draw or fade.

By 1935, Nelson had earned his first Masters invitation and won his first tournament. The Masters was to be his first major championship, though it was many years before the event earned this status. His first round 66 set a record, but more memorable was the way he caught Ralph Guldahl in the final round by playing the dread 12th and 13th in 2, 3 while Guldahl played this par 3 and par 5 in 5, 6.

But 1939 was his first great year. He won the prestigious Western Open, the North and South Tournament and the US Open. It was a long-drawn-out affair. Sam Snead should have won but took an 8 on the last and Nelson, Craig Wood and Densmore Shute tied. After 18 holes, Nelson and Wood were tied with 68s. Out they went again for another 18. Some say Nelson settled it when he holed a 1-iron shot for an eagle at the 4th hole.

Nelson's next major came in the 1940 US PGA, played as matchplay all through Nelson's career. Nelson proved in this championship that he was very good in matchplay. He got through to the final five times in seven years in the period 1939–45, winning for the second time in 1945. His other major championship was the Masters of 1942. After a tie on 280, he faced his exact contemporary and main rival in US golf, Ben Hogan, over an 18-hole play-off. Hogan jumped into an early lead and kept on playing well but Nelson pulled back to win with a 69 to Hogan's 70.

The pressure increased on Byron Nelson with each victory in that run of 11 in 1945. As the star attraction, he was required to spend a great deal of time helping to promote each tournament, attend lunches, cocktail parties and dinners, give press interviews and then go into the nearest town to do it all again for radio. But he kept on wanting to win, making last round charges that averaged out at $67\frac{1}{2}$ for the whole year. As he says today, 'Winners are different. They're a different breed of cat. They are willing to give of themselves whatever it takes to win.'

But Nelson couldn't keep on doing it. In 1946, he had only a moderately good year – by his standards. He won five times and tied for the US Open, losing the play-off by one stroke to Lloyd Mangrum on the second 18 holes of this marathon.

When Nelson announced his retirement, he gave pressures outside golf as his reason. Some said that his stomach was suffering or that his wife was a home-body who neither liked travelling around with Byron nor him being away from home on his own. It is not at all clear whether Nelson attempted comebacks but he did re-appear from time to time and showed that even he couldn't make the occasional appearance and win. However, he played consistently in the Masters for many years and won the 1951 Crosby. In 1955 he crossed the Atlantic to play in the Open Championship without great success but went on to the French Open and gave a brilliant exhibition of iron play on the way to his final victory.

LARRY NELSON

Larry Gene Nelson
(1947–   )
USA, was born in Fort
Payne, Alabama.
A self-effacing player capable
of major performances. He
won the US Open in 1983
and the US PGA in 1981
and 1987.

Most professional golfers have grooved their swing by around the age of 18 – but not Larry Nelson, one of the smoothest swingers in the golf business. He didn't try hitting a golf ball until he was 21. He went to a driving range one day, liked it and found hitting golf balls easy and he seemed to be good at it. A short time later he was working for a Georgia club pro and six months later turned professional. In 1974, he qualified to join the US Tour by playing in a tournament which was only the second time that Larry had taken part in a four round strokeplay event of any kind.

Nelson made money from the start – a tribute to the steadiness of his play through the green. His real breakthrough, however, came in 1979 when he won twice on the US Tour and raced up the money list to finish 2nd, behind Tom Watson. He hadn't been better than 26th in his previous five years. Nelson has not achieved as high a placing since, although he has won a great deal more money ($501,292 in 1987, for instance) than the $281,000 he accumulated in 1979.

His performance earned him his first Ryder Cup place and he made the most of it at The Greenbrier in West Virginia. He played in the maximum number of matches – five – and won the lot. What made this even more remarkable was that Seve Ballesteros, whom Nelson beat by 3 and 2 in their singles, was involved in four of the matches. Nelson again made the team in 1981 at Walton Heath, played four times, and again had a 100 per cent record. Perhaps Seve was pleased not to have been selected that year! After not qualifying for the next two US teams, there was considerable interest in how Nelson would do at Muirfield Village in 1987. The answer is, not so well: he lost two foursomes and a fourball but halved his singles with Bernhard Langer.

Dramatic though Nelson's early Ryder Cup results were, he is not a player who causes a great stir but goes about his business quietly and efficiently, astounding no one with power hitting but keeping the ball in play. He seems to be able to play most of a season unnoticed and then suddenly emerge with a victory. He has been very effective in major championships, which tend to reward consistency. His first came in 1981, and appropriately in his hometown of Atlanta. He won the US PGA by four strokes from Fuzzy Zoeller.

In 1983, Nelson had done nothing on the US Tour by the time June came round and the US Open at Oakmont. After two rounds, he was seven strokes behind but then produced a 65 which swept him up the field to one behind the lead which was held by Tom Watson and Ballesteros. With Seve fading, the event became largely a contest between Nelson and Watson but with just six players still left out on the course, play had to be abandoned because of severe thunderstorms. When play was resumed, Watson was on the 15th green and Nelson

Larry Nelson: an undramatic but consistent golfer

on the 16th tee. The pair were level. Nelson began by safely finding the green at this 226-yard hole. Even so, his 4-wood had not been a great shot and he was exactly 62 feet from the hole. Three putts stared him in the face. Instead, he holed it. He was in the lead and despite taking three putts on the last hole was champion, partly as a result of Watson faltering. Nelson had been 92nd on the US money list when the championship began and over half his season's winnings came from the US Open.

His third major came in 1987. This time it was the US PGA and again Nelson had done little all year. He went into the final round three off the lead but in a high scoring event his 72 was good enough to tie with Lanny Wadkins. He won the play-off by holing from about six feet while Wadkins missed from a little closer.

By the end of 1988 Larry Nelson had won ten times on the US Tour, where he has accumulated over $2\frac{1}{2}$ million, and twice in Japan.

JACK NICKLAUS

*Jack William Nicklaus
(1940–   )
USA, was born in
Columbus, Ohio.
One of the all-time greatest.
He won the Open
Championship in 1966, 1970
and 1978; the US Open in
1962, 1967, 1972 and 1980;
the Masters in 1963, 1965,
1966, 1972, 1975 and 1986;
the US PGA in 1963, 1971,
1973, 1975 and 1980 and the
US Amateur Championship
in 1959 and 1961.*

I'm understating the matter in writing that Jack Nicklaus has a real claim to be ranked highest of all in the Pantheon of golf's greatest. Many would say that there's not the slightest doubt of his supremacy. However, I prefer to stick by that old truism that all a golfer can do is beat the players of his own time. In Nicklaus's case, this is a truly remarkable period: 27 years elapsed between his first major, the 1959 US Amateur, and his Masters victory in 1986. No one comes really close to rivalling such longevity, not even Gary Player and Harold Hilton with 19 years and John Ball with 24. Put another way, Jack was the second youngest winner of the US Amateur – at $19\frac{1}{2}$ – and easily the oldest winner of the Masters at 46 years two months.

Only two players have won major professional championships at a greater age – Old Tom Morris, back in 1867, when about a month older than Nicklaus; and Julius Boros who was well into his 49th year when he won the 1968 US PGA Championship.

One can pick out many more achievements from Nicklaus's record which help to illustrate his status. Only two players have won any of the major championships six times: Harry Vardon in the Open Championship and Jack Nicklaus in the Masters. Bobby Jones, with 13, comes closest to Jack's unapproachable total of 20 majors. If one excludes amateur majors, Nicklaus's score is still impressive with a total of 18 as against 11 to Walter Hagen.

Others have won more tournaments – Gary Player, Sam Snead and Roberto de Vicenzo, for example. On the US Tour Nicklaus, with 71 wins, is second to Snead at 84. Though never highly active internationally Nicklaus has had 18 victories outside the USA, those mostly in Britain and Australia.

As a money-winner Nicklaus is unparalleled, with more than $5 million on the US Tour; with the rapid inflation of prize money he will soon be caught by Tom Watson. No one, however, is likely to equal his feat of being leading money-winner eight times which can be compared to five for Ben Hogan and Tom Watson and four for Arnold Palmer.

From his debut as a professional in January 1962 until 1980 Nicklaus started as favourite in nearly every event. Just two golfers in the twentieth century have been even more dominant – Bobby Jones and Ben Hogan – but in each case over a far shorter time span.

Nicklaus's golf game has evolved over the decades. He began as a player who simply overwhelmed golf courses with his power game; he has declared that his tactics were to hit his tee shots a very long way and then, using much more lofted clubs than most of his rivals, 'slop it on the green'. Once there, Nicklaus was one of the great putters of all time and the more vital the putt, the better he became.

There were weaknesses in his game. For a while, he was a relatively poor sand player and never became outstanding. He also lacked variety of shot from, say, 100 yards and closer. Surprisingly, consistency was also not one of Nicklaus's greatest strengths. In all his years on the US Tour, not once did he return the lowest annual stroke average.

Perhaps this last gives us a clue to one of Jack's main strengths: he seems to be able to produce his best when the demands on nerve and clear thinking are most intense. Of course, he has at times lost championships by hitting poor shots at the climax – the 1963 and 1977 Open Championships and the 1975 US Open are examples – but you will not find many more. Nicklaus has his own explanation. He believes he has been able to 'fail a little less' in the closing stages of a great event. Remember it is very seldom indeed that a run of birdies wins an event. Far more often the target over the last 40 minutes or so is two or three pars. How many have failed to get them?

Just as there have been relative weaknesses in Jack's playing techniques, there has been at least one in his competitive approach. It's almost absurd to say that he ought to have won more championships, but it really is so. In the 1960s and 1970s Jack went into all of them believing that he was the best player and ought to win. This 'ought' produced a defensive approach. He would begin by not attacking the course but instead played short of possible trouble with his tee shots or to safe areas of fairway. This approach sometimes meant that he had less chance of a birdie on a hole even though his par was safer. Quite frequently he left one of his prime weapons, the driver, in the bag except for use on the par 5s. As a result of these tactics Nicklaus, after two or three rounds, had usually managed to save the championship. However, he sometimes left himself with rather too much to do thereafter; a more thrilling Nicklaus then emerged. The driver came out of the bag and the shots to the green were fired straight at the flag. He swung into top gear when the situation looked serious.

Perhaps he favoured this approach because the cautious strategy had worked so well in his first Open Championship success at Muirfield in 1966. That year, Nicklaus decided that the rough was so severe and some of the bunkering so punitive that a softly, softly approach was needed. It paid off.

In contrast, when the championship returned to Muirfield in 1972, Jack was several strokes behind Trevino and Jacklin going into the final round. So brilliant was Nicklaus's play that he even took the lead at one point but, like Jacklin, was eventually thwarted by a couple of errors of his own and a chip-in from Trevino on the 71st hole.

Nicklaus, in his best years, saw off a considerable number of rivals to his supremacy. First there was the darling of the crowds, Arnold Palmer; then it appeared that Gary Player, Lee Trevino or Tom Weiskopf might inherit the crown – but only when they had very good years. Nicklaus managed to have a very good year every year. Then, for a couple of years, Johnny Miller, if mostly in US Tour events, produced golf of a quality that surpassed everyone. But it didn't last and Nicklaus kept going. Even late in his career, when overtaken by Tom Watson, he was able to revive himself after a disastrous 1979 and win both the US Open and the US PGA. In 1982 he deserved to win a record-breaking sixth US Open.

Surely that was that? When would he retire? Nicklaus fostered these thoughts by playing in events around the United States which he had ignored for years, as though he was showing himself for the last time. Then came the 1986 Masters victory.

Has he any remaining ambitions? Though he is so active in business and golf architecture, I suspect a few remain. No doubt a fifth US Open would delight him, or how about becoming the first man to win a major championship in his fifties?

OPPOSITE: *Nicklaus holes a vital putt during the final round of his sixth Masters in 1986*

155

NORMAN VON NIDA

*Norman George Von Nida
(1914–   )
Australia, was born in
Strathfield, Queensland.
Arguably the first Australian
to earn an international
reputation.*

When Norman Von Nida was playing golf during the 1930s, financial rewards in Australia were low. Von Nida mainly honed his game by playing countless money matches against amateurs off handicap. As Trevino said many years later, it's a hard school when you haven't got the money to pay up if you lose. Tournaments were few and far between and even if Britain beckoned, competitive golf didn't pay well there either. Von Nida's first excursion overseas was to the Philippines in 1938. The boat journey took three weeks but Von Nida won and did so again the following year.

Having beaten both Hagen and Sarazen when they toured Australia, Von Nida's sights were set on testing himself in Britain and the USA – but war threatened. He did make the long journey to the United States in 1939, but with little success. With the outbreak of war he returned to Australia and lost what should have been the peak golfing years of his late twenties and early thirties.

*Von Nida pictured during his
first visit to Britain in 1946*

By this time, he had won the Queensland title four times and the New South Wales twice and in 1946 set out for Britain. When the ship docked, Von Nida had £17 in his pocket but he soon added to it. He nearly won his first tournament and soon afterwards won a News Chronicle event. His sights, though, were set on the glory of the Open Championship. He led the qualifiers over 36 holes but, after a good first round, couldn't produce his best golf afterwards. He finished tied for 4th place behind champion Sam Snead and had good cause to remember his play on the feared Road Hole. He had a couple of 3s and two par 4s. I wonder if anyone has managed the hole any better in four competitive rounds? His British season as a whole, however, was profitable. Only Locke did better for money-winnings. Von Nida – how times have changed – won £1,330!

By this time, all the main features of the little Australian's game were well established. Among the great players of his day, he was unusual in almost always relying on straight hitting rather than being either a right-to-left or left-to-right player. Von Nida thought this made him specially effective in a wind. Though not a long hitter (he couldn't usually make the par 5s in two strokes), he kept the ball on the fairway and was an outstanding pitcher of the ball. Gary Player rated him the best bunker player he had ever seen. Norman was a good, but by no means outstanding, putter until he succumbed to the yips in late career.

He returned to Australia to win the New South Wales Championship again and his first major Australian title, the PGA. His greatest season followed – in Britain in 1947. In one spell, he won four out of six entries and in the season as a whole (one with relatively few events compared to today) won or tied for 1st, seven times. He was far and away the leading money-winner and his total of £3,263 broke the previous record by about £750.

The Open Championship was once more his target. He was the clear favourite and led the qualifiers. After three rounds of the championship proper he shared the lead but was one of those caught by a late wind. It was Fred Daly's year, and Von Nida tied 6th.

His 1948 season was less successful. Again the Open escaped him but he tied for 3rd place and also won the prestigious Dunlop Masters at Sunningdale. During it, he broke the course record with a 63 which stood for many years. Von Nida won three further British events, the last in 1951. In Australia, he won the PGA four times and took the Australian Open Championship in 1950, 1952 and 1953.

Sometimes fatalistic, Von Nida had always felt that a golfer was finished at 40. In this case, his putting nerve had gone. In later life he was always ready to help up-and-coming players and such men as Peter Thomson, Bruce Crampton, Kel Nagle, David Graham and Greg Norman benefited from his advice.

GREG NORMAN

*Gregory John Norman
(1955–   )
Australia, was born in Mount
Isa, Queensland.*
*Though a modern superstar he
has so far failed to make full
impact in the major
championships. He won the
Open Championship in
1986.*

Major championships have always been difficult to win. Walter Hagen once commented that you could have a good or lucky week and win one, but you had to be great to win two. As you can see, Norman still has just his great Turnberry performance – when he played in the worst of the weather on the two bad days of the championship – to his name in the majors, though he has often come very close (one shot less would have done it) on a number of occasions. Though Greg has the right looks and has cultivated his image carefully he is not young in golfing terms. Aged 34 early in 1989, his best chances may lie in the past unless he could have another 1986 but this time win the lot. That did not seem likely at Augusta in 1989. Once more, Greg took a bogey 5 on the very last hole to lose his opportunity to join Nick Faldo and Scott Hoch in the sudden death play-off. Normally so cooperative with the press, he declined interview afterwards.

When he came to Turnberry in 1986, he had lost the Masters by blocking his iron shot to the last green 20 yards into the crowds on the right and tied for 2nd behind Jack Nicklaus. In the US Open, he was in the lead after both second and third rounds but his 75 on the last day was easily the worst score from anyone in contention. Norman said he had not felt in the mood. The course at Turnberry seemed to have been arranged so that the low-scoring feats of Watson and Nicklaus in 1977 could not be repeated. The fairways were very narrow and the rough often knee high and thick. Balls could also disappear from sight in greenside areas. Then, on the first day, the winds blew. The favourite, Seve Ballesteros took 76. Many scored a lot higher. Norman kept himself in the championship with a 74. Only about a dozen others did better.

On the second day, though it was cloudy and chilly, the winds were light. Norman cut loose. Only the soft greens helped scoring but his 63 equalled the championship record (and included three putts on the 18th green!). It gave him a two-stroke lead which was cut to one on a chilly, wet third day. Out last the final day with Tsuneyuki Nakajima, he may well have been encouraged when the Japanese three-putted the 1st for a 6. On the 3rd, Norman suddenly found himself with the large margin of five strokes when he holed a 40-yard bunker shot for a birdie 3. Norman was round in a very composed 69, his lead never threatened. He won by five from Gordon J. Brand of Yorkshire.

Less than a month later it looked as though Greg might win a second major championship, the US PGA, which was played at Inverness. He jumped into a first round lead with a 65 and rounds of 68 and 69 left him four strokes ahead at the end of each day. Going into the final day the field was six and more strokes away – with one exception. That was Bob Tway, who had beaten Norman's new course record with a

64. He was a distant threat, four strokes behind and unlikely to produce such a low-scoring round the next day.

As Tway and Norman played the 11th, the gap was still four strokes. At the 11th, however, Norman began to let Tway in, pitching into a bunker and ending up with a double bogey 6. He followed with a couple of quick hook tee shots and the pair were level after the 14th. The position remained the same as they played the last. Norman then seemed to have made a decisive move with far the better tee shot. He was in the fairway, Tway well to the right in the rough. Tway had no chance of holding the green with his second shot. Instead, he bunkered it short on the right and Norman's approach unluckily spun back from the putting surface into thick grass on the fringe. Tway had an easy enough bunker shot and was about 15 yards from the hole. He expected to get it close but not hole out – but that is what he did, virtually for the championship.

Of course, the events on the 18th were agonisingly bad luck for Norman but Tway had only succeeded in doing what all good bunker players have in mind when faced with a straightforward sand shot. Norman had lost because he had three bogeys and two double bogeys on his card *before* they played the 18th.

For Greg, the 1987 Masters was to be genuinely unlucky. After an untidy first 36 holes, he swept up the field with a 66 to be one behind the leader. After a steady round the final day he had a putt of about five yards to win and missed by an inch. Playing off with Seve

Ballesteros and Larry Mize, he hit his second shot onto the 10th dead at the flag. It could have stopped dead but ran to the rear fringe. When Seve took three putts, he was out of it. Mize and Norman moved to the 11th, a par 4 of 455 yards with a small lake posing a threat to the left of the green. This is the hole that Ben Hogan was referring to when he said: 'If you ever see me on the green with my second, you'll know I missed my shot'. His aim was to keep well away from the lake and finish just off the green to the right.

If that was Larry Mize's policy as well, he overdid it. He missed the green to the right by some 20 yards and was nearly 50 yards from the hole. He would need great skill and a little luck as well to make a par 4. With the door wide open, Norman Hogan-ed his approach correctly, finishing on the fringe to the right. In the circumstances, it was a good enough shot to win the Masters but, as the world knows, it didn't because Mize freaked his pitch-and-run into the hole.

The ones you don't win don't count, so Norman still has just the one major championship on his record. This casts some doubt over his status as a superstar, even though he enjoyed a long spell at the top of the Sony rankings. There are no doubts at all, however, that he is a superstar as an international tournament golfer. He had his first win, in Australia, in 1976. That was only the fourth time he had entered a tournament and the victories have since followed in a steady flow. Certainly in his home country he remains the dominant figure with a total of 22 wins which include the Australian PGA twice, four Australian Masters titles and the Australian Open in 1980, 1985 and 1987.

He began serving an apprenticeship on the European Tour in 1977 and was soon a tournament winner. By the end of 1988 he had 15 wins, including the Open Championship and three World Matchplay titles. He was 2nd on the money list in 1980 and 1st in 1982.

Greg had cautiously taken his time before committing himself to the US Tour which he began to play in 1983. He now has five wins and over $2\frac{1}{4}$ million. His biggest year was 1986 when he won some $650,000 and had two wins – plus those near misses in all three majors. Norman then came over to Europe to win the European Open, take team and individual honours in the Dunhill Cup and win the World Matchplay. Off he went to Australia and had three victories in a row. This is one of the great winning sequences in golf history.

Norman's early successes were based on power and he remains perhaps the best long straight driver in the world. I thought a weakness in his play was that he seemed to need to hit every shot from driver to wedge more or less flat out. However, in the mid-1980s he had a series of lessons and dramatically improved his close-range shot-making and made good use of what he called 'soft knees', keeping them relaxed and flowing with the stroke. Norman has always been a good putter but deadly holing out of those missable putts was a major factor in his 1986 performances.

CHRISTY O'CONNOR

To call Christy O'Connor a natural golfer is a sure way of annoying him. The truth of the matter is that O'Connor practised just about as much as anyone as a young man. So, probably, did most of those who, as mature golfers, gained a reputation for spending little time on the practice ground. O'Connor in later years was simply one of those who had established his swing and preferred to do no more than hit warm-up shots before playing a tournament round. Despite aches and pains, he had one original excuse: overdoing the practice shots, he claimed, made him feel too loose and relaxed and he played the worse for it.

In making my selection of the 100 greatest golfers, I have had players' successes in the major championships constantly in mind. O'Connor won none of them, though he came within a hair's-breadth of the Open Championship. Despite this omission I cannot for a moment rank him behind a fluke performer such as Andy North who has won just three events in his career, two of which happened to be the US Open.

There was only one club that Christy O'Connor never managed to master: this was the putter, with which he had a quick, rather snatchy

Christy O'Connor (1924–) Ireland, was born in Galway. Often been called one of the most 'natural' golfers ever.

Christy O'Connor plays a shot at Stoneham in 1961. If you have a fluid swing like Christy, your game lasts

method. I know of no one else, however, who had more variety of shots through the rest of the bag. There is one legendary story about his ability as a shot-maker. He was playing a practice round with a young professional. The young pro walloped an 8-iron onto the green of a par 3. O'Connor followed by floating in a 5-iron. The young pro observed that an 8 was all he had needed. O'Connor called a halt for a demonstration, hitting the green with every club in the bag from a putter to the driver. That, my friends, is shot-making. It involved a range of skills from toeing in the pitching irons and taking the loft away by hitting with the hands well ahead of the clubhead at impact, to floating in high slices (or just hitting very gently) with the power clubs.

Because O'Connor didn't win a tournament on mainland Britain until he was past 30, he sounds like a late developer. The fact of the matter is that O'Connor couldn't afford the expense of crossing the Irish sea. However, his first win happened to coincide with the arrival of the first £1,000 cheque. By coincidence, many years later he also won the first five figure prize, when his victory total was past 20. From 1955 to 1970, he was never lower than 10th in the money list and was 2nd seven times.

To this day, Christy feels cheated of the 1958 Open Championship. He was in the lead after rounds of 67 and 68 but played behind Peter Thomson on the final day. He considers that the Australian deliberately played slowly to unsettle him. Be that as it may, Christy lost concentration and fell away to a 73, which left him three off the lead, which was held now by Thomson. O'Connor, although still delayed, managed to concentrate better in the afternoon. He came to the last hole with Leopoldo Ruiz from Argentina with a chance of outright victory – if he could get a 3. The 18th at Lytham measured 379 yards and on the final day O'Connor decided to attack it with a drive and a wedge. There was a hold-up, not Thomson's fault this time, but the marshals failed to prevent the spectators from flooding onto the 18th fairway. Tired of waiting, O'Connor decided to aim at the bunkers along the left but play short with a 3-wood. Alas, he reached them and the 5 which resulted left him one stroke away from the Thomson/ Thomas play-off.

Christy O'Connor was my partner in many Ryder Cup matches and was selected for the team a record ten times from 1955 to 1973. He was also in the Irish World Cup pair 15 times and won the title for Ireland, partnered by Harry Bradshaw, in 1958. When his tournament days were over, O'Connor won the British PGA Seniors title six times in eight years from 1976 and also won the World Seniors in 1976 and 1977.

MARK O'MEARA

Mark O'Meara won his only major the hard way, defeating the previous year's champion, John Cook, in the final. The same year, 1979, he won the Californian and Mexican titles. Like many top amateurs, both British and American, he allowed himself no time to make further impact in the amateur game and, without a Walker Cup appearance, turned professional in 1980. In 1981, his first year on the Tour, he was soon making money and came close to his first win, losing a play-off for the Tallahassie Open. He finished 55th on the money list and was Rookie of the Year.

Many find adjusting to professional golf takes time, and though O'Meara was winning money and good opinions, his first victory was delayed until 1984. That year, his consistency was highly impressive

Mark Francis O'Meara (1957–)
USA, was born in Goldsboro, North Carolina. A leading US Tour player, he has also been successful internationally. He won the US Amateur Championship in 1979.

Mark O'Meara could suddenly break out of the pack to become number one in America

for he also had five 2nd places and the most top ten finishes on the Tour – 15. His prize money total, $465,873, was only just behind Tom Watson's.

O'Meara has not finished as high as that 2nd money place since and he is one of the players I have selected more on grounds of his potential than of his achievements. Curtis Strange took a long time to become a star, so may O'Meara. There are several things that I particularly admire about his game: his putting stroke looks entirely natural and relaxed while he has a range of shots through the green; he doesn't rely on one basic pattern. O'Meara prefers to draw the ball with his woods for additional length but to fade his irons to get more control and a softer landing on the greens. When I have watched him play, I have always been impressed by the good pace and rhythm of his swing and, as Ben Hogan once said of Lee Trevino, 'I love to watch the way he uses his hands'.

In 1985, O'Meara achieved the quite rare feat of winning back-to-back tournaments – the early season Bing Crosby National Pro-Am, as it was still known then, and the Hawaiian Open. His success ensured Ryder Cup selection where he played on the losing US team at The Belfry. An early US Tour win in 1989 makes it likely that he will be back again.

Mark O'Meara didn't win on the US Tour between these victories but he has been far more willing to compete internationally than many of his fellow US Tour players. In 1985 he won the Fuji Sankei Classic in Japan and the Kapalua International in Hawaii. The following year he took the Australian Masters and in 1987 the Lawrence Batley International.

In 1988 he tied 3rd in the US Open and tied 9th in the US PGA. His career earnings in the US have surpassed $2 million.

FRANCIS OUIMET

The US Golf Association venerates the history of golf. The main reason that the US Open was played at The Country Club in Brookline in 1963 and in 1988 was in recognition of the 50th and 75th anniversaries of Ouimet's famous victory. I can think of no other examples in major championships when this has been done.

Ouimet (pronounced 'Wimmit') was a 20-year-old shop assistant when he took part in that far-off Open. He was not renowned even in amateur golf and had been knocked out of the US Amateur in the second round that year, having failed to qualify for the matchplay stages three times previously. In his preparations for the event, Ouimet was hardly able to break 90 but suddenly it all changed. He had the second best score in the two qualifying rounds but when the championship proper began, Ouimet started extremely shakily – 6, 6, 5 – but recovered to finish with a very respectable 77. His 74 in the second round brought him to four off the lead and with a 74 in the third he drew level with the English champions Harry Vardon and Ted Ray.

None of the three produced a good final round, Ouimet least of all. He went to the turn in 43 but then improved. With four holes to play, he needed to be one under the par to tie. His birdie came at the 17th, from a long putt, and he was finally left with a yard putt on the last. He knocked it in as if on a casual practice round. The cheers rang out long and loud. But, of course, no one thought that he had a chance of beating Vardon and Ray in a play-off over 18 holes the next day. On the first nine, Ouimet was never more than a stroke worse than Vardon and levelled when he pitched dead at the 8th. All three turned in 38 and Ouimet went ahead on the 10th when he was the only one to par the hole. At the 12th, he moved two ahead. On the 15th Ray went out, with a 6 to 4s from Vardon and Ouimet; Vardon was disposed of on the 17th. He bunkered his tee shot and took 5, while Ouimet holed a good putt for a 3.

When it was all over, Ouimet had gone round in 72 to Vardon's 77 and Ray's 78. Ouimet said, 'I simply tried my best to keep this cup from going to our friends across the water. I am very glad to have been the agency for keeping the cup in America.' His victory showed Americans that they could compete with the British, and it did the cause of golf no harm at all that Ouimet did not come from a country club golfing background. It was far and away Ouimet's greatest achievement though he was more pleased to win the US Amateur Championship the following year. He won again in 1931, when approaching 40.

Ouimet never seriously considered turning professional though the USGA did take away his amateur status because they thought he was

Francis de Sales Ouimet (1893–1967)
USA, was born in Brookline, Massachusetts.
His victory in the 1913 US Open changed a golfing nation's image of itself. He won the 1913 US Open and the US Amateur Championship in 1914 and 1931.

Francis Ouimet seen a few years after he had beaten Vardon and Ray in the play-off for the 1913 US Open

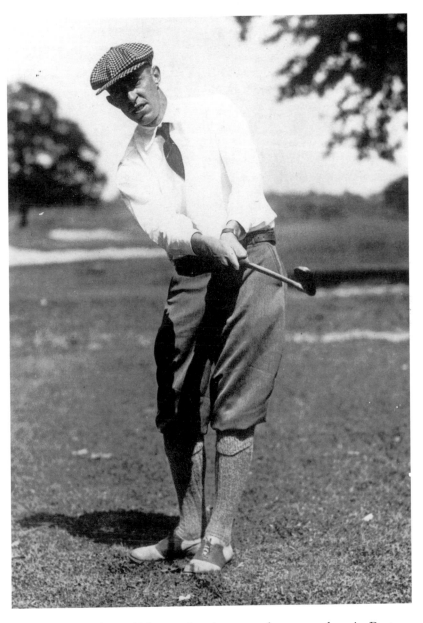

profiting from his golf fame when he opened a sports shop in Boston in 1916. After the First World War, the USGA relented. One result was that, many years later in 1951, Ouimet was able to become the first American captain of the R and A. A far greater amateur golfer, Bobby Jones, was a more obvious choice but he had profited mightily from his golfing status after his 1930 retirement.

ARNOLD PALMER

Golf is a game which demands great self-control, even more so perhaps for players of the modern era. You can't hit your opponent if he holes a 30-yard putt, nor should you throw your putter over the railway line as Norman Von Nida once did at Southport and Ainsdale some 30 years ago. Even breaking your own property – an ineffective putter, for example – is much frowned on. If you indulge in the cheating tolerated in so many other sports you will find yourself banned for life from either professional or club golf. All this means that players have to contain their emotions. For the most part, they do this very well indeed – and it can make them seem very dull fellows.

Palmer, however, was a man who showed his emotions, his joys and his agonies, without ever overstepping the bounds of what is considered correct golf course behaviour. The crowds (the so-called Arnie's Army) flocked to follow him and the television ratings soared in the United States. In Britain his finishes of 2nd, 1st, 1st in the Open Championships of 1960, 1961 and 1962 did a very great deal to revive international interest in the event and sparked the mass American invasion that was to follow in a few years.

The story begins in 1947 when Palmer won the Western Pennsylvania Amateur. In 1953 he won the Ohio Amateur but began to become a national figure in 1954 after service with the US Coast Guard and time at Wake Forest University. That year he won the US Amateur and soon after turned professional. His first US Tour victory came in 1955 – the Canadian Open – and the following two seasons he won six more. The first major was not far away. In 1958 he won the Masters, something he made a habit of doing in alternate years, sometimes throwing one away in between.

Other tournament wins continued to come his way and in 1960, his greatest year, the floodgates opened. He won eight times. His Masters win helped to create his reputation of always being able to mount a last round charge. Of course he couldn't manage it every time, but when he could they were memorable. This time he birdied the last two holes to catch and overtake Ken Venturi. Events at Cherry Hills in the US Open that year undoubtedly added to the legend. Palmer went in the final round six off the lead, apparently determined to get himself a 65 because '280 totals win US Opens'. One key was the 1st, a shortish par 4 Arnold thought he could drive. In trying to prove it he had dropped three strokes in the championship. This time, a savage blow reached and he two-putted for a birdie. He went on to birdie the next three as well. Out in 30, he had caught the field and parred his way home to win by a couple of strokes as players such as the young amateur Jack Nicklaus and the ageing Titan, Ben Hogan made errors. It was certainly one of the great last round charges in golf's history.

Arnold Daniel Palmer (1929–   ) USA, was born in Latrobe, Pennsylvania.

The most charismatic figure in modern golf. He won the US Amateur Championship in 1954, the Masters in 1958, 1960, 1962 and 1964, the US Open in 1960 and the Open Championship in 1961 and 1962.

Arnold Palmer playing at Birkdale in 1965, a year in which I played two fourballs against him. Oddly, although he remained a terrific player for half-a-dozen years more, he had already won his last major

Off to St Andrews for the Open Championship and, with two already under his belt, a chance to pursue the Holy Grail of a grand slam of all four major titles. After three good rounds, he was still four strokes behind the steady Australian Kel Nagle. Palmer began with two exact pitch shots and two birdies but both reached the turn in 34 – the gap was the same four strokes. At the 13th, Palmer became a threat with a 3 to a bogey 5. Nothing much changed until the dreaded 17th. Here Palmer got his first par of the week and then birdied the relatively easy last hole. Nagle, just behind, finished with two pars and that was good enough. But it had been another memorable Palmer charge.

He made another one the following year in the US Masters. Gary Player led him by four strokes going into the final round but as Palmer faced his 7-iron shot to the final green he knew he had done it. A par was all he needed. He sent that shot into a bunker, thinned his next through the green and eventually took a double bogey 6.

And so to his second Open Championship at Birkdale. This was largely played in abominable weather and, in a full gale on the second day, he managed to birdie five of the first six holes. It was simply superhuman golf, perhaps the greatest burst Palmer ever played. There was another great moment in the next round. Playing the 16th, then a par 5 of 510 yards, Palmer hit his third shot almost out of bounds into deep rough at the foot of willow scrub. He gave a full lash at his ball with a sand iron, carved through everything and up and up his ball flew to finish stone-dead by the hole. In the end he only won by a stroke from Dai Rees but was always in command of the championship.

After another Masters the following year he gave his best ever performance in a major championship at Troon. Kel Nagle was the only player who kept in touch and he finished six strokes away. Palmer set an Open Championship record with his 276 over a hard, fast-running burned-up course that hardly suited his style of play. The next men were 13 strokes behind.

He was god both sides of the Atlantic. Yet Palmer never again contended strongly for an Open Championship and was only to win one other major, his fourth Masters in 1964.

Several times he came close to another US Open and, in particular, 'Olympic 1966' may prove to be engraved on his heart. He was seven strokes ahead of Casper with nine to play but Casper caught him as Palmer made error after error. They tied and Casper won the play-off, again after Palmer had a good lead.

On the US Tour, Palmer remained a formidable force up to 1971. By that time he had won 60 events and added a final victory in 1973. From 1958 to 1971 he was never worse than 10th on the money list. He was leading money-winner four times and for another five years was in the top three. But Palmer was always more interested in winning than in the money and in that respect ranks below only Snead, Nicklaus and Hogan. He also had 19 overseas wins.

Arnold Palmer in sand during the 1987 Masters

Palmer made golf appear an exciting game. His swing may have been in full control but it didn't look like it. He gave a furious lash at the ball and, as Henry Cotton once remarked, never finished balanced or in the same position twice. The reason was that Palmer, a natural hooker, always drove through the ball with his right hand, striving to prevent its turning over too soon. The result was a high but unnatural looking follow-through. Nevertheless, he was an excellent driver of the ball, very long but not quite as long as the effort expended made it seem. He was even better with the long irons but a relatively mediocre pitcher of the ball and bunker player. On the greens in his great years he gave the impression of charging everything, brashly confident that he could hole any three-to-five-footers coming back. His knock-kneed stance and still head were much imitated. His decline was mainly caused by loss of confidence on the greens and some think that the bold play which had won him such a massive following became more cautious.

However, perhaps too much has been made of the sad decline of Palmer. After all, he won majors into his mid-thirties and important events into the mid-forties, remaining a force on the US Tour to about the same time. His only failure is not quite to rank with the three or four greatest of all time. That's a small failure.

CALVIN PEETE

Calvin Peete
(1943–   )
USA, was born in Detroit,
Michigan.
One of the most accurate
players ever through the green.

Although Peete has won no major championships and, in his mid-forties is unlikely to do so, he did win the 1985 Tournament Players' Championship. This is the event that US Tour commissioner Deane Beman has been trying to promote as a fifth major for several years.

Peete was a late developer in many ways. For a start, he is one of the few players of this day and age who didn't have his first swing with a golf club at the age of six or earlier. Peete thought golf was a rich man's game and rather a silly one at that; however, it was obvious that Jack Nicklaus was making a fortune from his golfing skills. Peete played his first game at age 23 and five years later, in 1971, he turned professional. He joined the US Tour in 1976 when he was well into his thirties.

Having barely covered his expenses for a few years, Peete became a winner in 1979 and never looked back. His peak years were from 1982

The US Tour statistics
showed Peete that although he
had the steadiest long game on
the circuit, he was a poor
putter. He soon put that right

to 1986 when he was three times among the top four money-winners and was a member of two Ryder Cup teams. He has 12 wins on the US Tour to his credit and one in Japan in a period when such a tally has become rare indeed.

Besides the disadvantages of starting late, Peete also brought a physical handicap to the game. He fell out of a tree as a child and, like former US Open champion Ed Furgol, cannot straighten his left elbow so that any theories about the importance of the straight left arm have to go out of the window. It is perhaps as a result of this that Peete is a relatively short hitter. He makes up for it by regularly heading the US Tour statistics for percentage of fairways hit and is nearly as impressive at finding the greens. When Peete first noticed how well he was rating in these areas of the game, he realised that his putting was a great deal less effective. Practising his putting may well have been the key to his best years which have brought him more than $2 million on the US Tour. Calvin Peete must also be the best black golfer ever and for a while in the 1980s had a claim to be considered the most effective tournament competitor operating in the United States.

There are, perhaps, two principal reasons for his remarkable tee-to-green consistency. One is, simply, that Peete is no power player. The angles and averages certainly mean that he will hit and hold more fairways than a Norman or a Calcavecchia, who let rip at everything. This is not the whole story, however. Peete is beautifully balanced through the hitting area – and there are many players who can't claim that.

GARY PLAYER

*Gary Jim Player
(1935–   )
South Africa, was born in
Johannesburg.
His major championship
record in the post-Second
World War period is second
only to Jack Nicklaus's. He
won the Open Championship
in 1959, 1968 and 1974, the
US Open in 1965, the US
PGA in 1962 and 1972 and
the Masters in 1961, 1974
and 1978.*

Gary Player was born a natural athlete but he had to make himself into a golfer. When he first came to play in Britain in 1955, several well-meaning pros were quite outspoken when Gary asked their advice on his prospects. We (I was one of them) thought that he should go back home, find a job and play golf for fun. Why was this? Well, Gary had a hooker's grip, and a very flat swing. Worse, he had little balance or rhythm and no apparent feel for the game. At the time, we perhaps didn't notice his tenacity and how good he was around the greens.

In a sense, we were not quite as far wrong as history makes us seem; Gary Player has never appeared a world-class golfer with the long clubs when he is hitting flat out. It's only from, say, the 5-iron down that he has ever really looked the part. He has, however, pursued success with more desire than anyone else in the history of golf. He worked hard on his game. First he completely changed his left-hand grip from four knuckles showing to none, and eventually, after consultations with the guru Ben Hogan, settled for left thumb straight down the shaft and the right set in a slightly weak position. As a result of his fairly flat swing, his bad shots continued mostly to miss fairways on the left. While Player was still making these modifications he had already made himself outstanding at the short pitch, chipping, bunker play and putting. He always seemed to be able to get down in two from sand, possibly as a result of those thousands of hours spent practising, when his aim was to hole a number of bunker shots before going home.

That splendid short game and will to win brought Player success long before he had sorted out his long game. In Britain, he had his first victory in 1956 and was South African Open champion the same year. In 1957 he was off to the United States – then the centre of the golf world – and to Australia also, where he beat Peter Thomson in the final of the PGA Championship. The next year, he took the Australian Open and the first of his 21 tournaments in the USA. In 1959 he won the Open Championship at Muirfield. When the last day's 36 holes began, he was eight strokes behind the leader but his rounds of 70 and 68 were the best and he won by two.

In 1961 he became the first overseas golfer to head the US money-winning list and the first to win the Masters, a victory partly given him by Arnold Palmer. Player bunkered his second shot to the last but still got his par 4. Behind, Arnold Palmer needed a par to win. He drove well and allowed himself to think the tournament was finished. Concentration faltering, he too bunkered his second shot, thinned his recovery through the green and took three more to hole out. There was another first for Gary the following year. Having lost his Masters title to Palmer in a play-off, he later became the first overseas player to win the US PGA.

In 1965, Gary set another landmark. With his US Open victory at Bellerive, he was the first overseas golfer since Ted Ray in 1920 to win that championship and one of only four golfers to win all four majors (Jack Nicklaus, Gene Sarazen and Ben Hogan are the others). Player now wanted to be the first to do this Grand Slam twice and to hold his position, with Nicklaus and Palmer, as one of the Big Three. Player never managed that second slam because he failed to win a second US Open title, but he continued to add major championships to his record.

In 1968, he won seven times worldwide and took the Open Championship a second time, winning a very tense head-to-head duel with Jack Nicklaus at Carnoustie. The weather was highly unpleasant – ideal for Gary, who sought out bad weather in South Africa to accustom himself to playing in it. This very good year stopped the tongues which were saying that Player, in his mid-thirties, was burned out.

Much the same thing happened in 1974 when he was close to 40. It was to be the only year in which Player won two major championships. The first of these was his second Masters and he did it in remarkable fashion. After two rounds he was five behind but brought himself back

Player v Palmer at Wentworth in 1964. Player lost to Palmer but went on to win the title five times

Gary Player seen hitting flat out. As so often, his finish isn't textbook

into contention with a 66. With nine holes to play as many as eight players might have won it but Gary settled the outcome with a 9-iron second shot to inches on the 17th green which put him two ahead.

At Lytham in the Open Championship he gave one of his most dominant performances. In severe winds, his opening rounds of 69 and 68 gave him a two-stroke lead over Peter Oosterhuis and he held on to win by four, despite a frantic search for his ball on the 17th in the final round, and hitting his second shot to the last against the clubhouse wall. During the year, he took his victory total worldwide to 100 and finished off with a round of 59 in the Brazilian Open.

Was this Player's last hurrah? Not a bit of it. In 1978, when most observers felt that he would be putting his feet up, he had one of his best years. First came a third and most remarkable Masters victory, which contained perhaps the greatest final round charge in the event. It was a 64 but for quite some time nothing very dramatic happened. Player reached the turn in 34 but he had begun seven behind the leader, Hubert Green. He then birdied six holes on the homeward nine and one by one those playing behind failed to match his total. Greatly encouraged, he won the next two events on the US Tour and came within sight of making it four in a row.

Player is the most successful overseas-based golfer ever to compete on the US Tour and internationally. He has, for instance, an amazing 30 wins in Australia to his credit, including their Open Championship on seven occasions, and five victories in the Wentworth Matchplay Championship, where he proved himself the best matchplay golfer of the modern era. He won the South African Open a record 13 times, eclipsing even Bobby Locke.

Throughout his career, Gary Player was a highly adept self-publicist. His black uniform made him readily identifiable and provided good copy when he said that he wore black because it absorbed the sun's rays and made him stronger. His dietary tastes of bananas, raisins, wheat germ and no alcohol, tea or coffee were newsworthy, as was his regime of press-ups, running, bodybuilding and his claim that 'the more I practise, the luckier I get'.

JUDY RANKIN

Golfers are probably fortunate among top sports performers in not being laid low too often by serious injuries. Damage is often caused to wrists, tendons and elbows by constant impact with the turf, but the area which suffers the worst harm is the lower back. Injuries can be caused by the twisting movement in the golf swing, particularly when a player has a shut-face action. Judy Rankin did have such an action and it brought her career to a premature end. In a very few years, her back was the main reason why she rapidly slipped down the money lists and now, though only into her early forties, she has played little or no tournament golf for several years.

Judy Rankin was one of the most precocious of stars. At the age of 14 she won the Missouri state title and was leading amateur in the US Open the following year. Missouri title-winner again in 1961, she was

Judy Rankin (née Torluemke) (1945–   )
USA, was born in St Louis, Missouri.
One of the most successful LPGA players during the 1970s.

Who says you can't play golf with a strong left-hand grip?

179

also twice a semi-finalist in the US Junior Championship in both 1960 and 1961. In 1962, and still only 17 years old, she turned professional. Success did not come immediately but by the mid-1960s she had established herself and in 1968 she won the first tournament of her career total of 26. In 1970 she won again and victories followed thick and fast thereafter until her last in 1979.

From 1965 to 1979, she had 11 placings in the top nine of money-winners and twice led the field – in 1976 and 1977. These were also her best years as a tournament winner. She took six events in 1976 and five the following year. A couple of years later, she stood 2nd on the all-time money-winners list. The rises in prize money have long meant that her status in this respect has declined but all those wins still count.

Consistency was a hallmark of Judy Rankin's career and in 1977 she set a record (which still stands) of 25 times finishing in the top ten in a total of 28 tournament entries.

With a very strong left hand grip, it's no surprise that Judy hit a low draw from the tee. She was extremely proficient with the fairway woods, partly because she was no power player so they were much in use. She was an excellent putter and became a familiar face in Britain as a result of twice winning the Colgate European Open, in 1974 and 1977.

TED RAY

'Hit it a bloody sight harder, mate.' That, long ago, was Ted Ray's advice to a club golfer who was enquiring how he could get more distance on his tee shots. Ted Ray was certainly a hard hitter himself. He amazed the young Bobby Jones during a 1913 exhibition tour of the United States with Harry Vardon. Jones respected the rhythm of Vardon and the fact that he seemed to par all the holes but Ray – what a clout he gave the ball!

At the time, Ray had emerged as the possible successor to the Great Triumvirate of Harry Vardon, James Braid and J.H. Taylor, all several years older than he. When in his mid-twenties, Ray reached the final of the PGA Matchplay Championship, barely second in status to the Open Championship at the time. Soon after, he began making his mark in the Open and had four finishes in the top six from 1907 to 1911.

The next year, 1912, he took the first round lead with a 71 at Muirfield and a 73 to follow increased the strength of his position at the head of the field. Unthreatened, Ray played out the last day with rounds of 76 and 75. He won by four strokes from Harry Vardon

Edward Ray (1877–1943) England, was born in Jersey. One of only three British-based players to win both the Open Championship and the US Open. He won the Open Championship in 1912 and the US Open in 1920.

Ted Ray, pipe in mouth, pictured during the Open in 1923. He nearly always allowed his feet to swivel round

with the next man home, James Braid, another four away. Ray's 295 aggregate equalled the second best ever scored in the championship.

The following year, he went on the tour of the United States with Vardon. Their play was in great contrast: Vardon all accuracy through the green but a nervous holer-out, while Ray was the prodigious hitter of the day and apt to find himself a long way off target at times. His recovery play, however, was excellent and he was a fine putter. In the US Open that year, both Vardon and Ray were expected to walk away with the championship but played poorly. This gave other players a chance and the one who took it was the 20-year-old American amateur, Francis Ouimet. The three of them tied and Ouimet played the round of his life to beat both the Englishmen in the 18-hole play-off.

There was ample revenge for Ray on his next trip to the United States in 1920 when he became the last British player to win the US Open until Tony Jacklin in 1970. After two rounds Ray lay a couple of strokes off the lead. On the morning of the final day, Vardon took the initiative with a 71 to lead by a stroke with Ray three behind. This was a championship Vardon should have won, even at the age of 50. After 11 holes, he had a four-stroke advantage but, no doubt tiring during his second round of the day, could not cope in the storm which then sprang up. This gave Ray, and others, a chance. Ray made a good start, gaining a stroke on par over the first six holes and then getting his fourth straight birdie of the championship on the 7th. This was a dog-leg par 4 of some 320 yards. Ray chose to ignore the dog-leg and sent successive drives soaring over everything to the heart of the green. He lost strokes to par thereafter but finished with a total one better than Vardon's.

Behind, both Leo Diegel and Jock Hutchison were well placed to better Ray's total but both fell away. At 43 Ray was the oldest man to win the US Open and that record stood until Ray Floyd's success at Shinnecock Hills in 1986 at the age of 44.

Ted Ray played in the first Britain versus USA match in 1921 and again in 1926 and 1927, when he was playing captain at the age of 50.

DAI REES

Some golfers earn labels for which they must come to feel a profound distaste. Sam Snead, for example, goes into golf history as the great player who failed to win the US Open. Three British golfers, despite their eminence in the game, are reduced in stature by lacking an Open Championship on their records. They are Abe Mitchell, my father Percy Alliss and Dai Rees.

The young Rees appeared as a sudden comet in the days when golfers didn't seem to reach maturity until about the age of 30. The stage was the PGA Matchplay Championship of 1936. Rees reached the final and met E.R. Whitcombe, runner-up in the 1924 Open Championship. At lunch Rees was five down after the morning's 18 holes. By the 29th he had squared and went on to win. He was champion again in 1938 and after the war continued to have a remarkable record in the event, beating Henry Cotton and Frank Jowle in the finals of 1949 and 1950. Rees went on to reach three more finals and in the last two, 1967 and 1969, was 54 and 56 years old. These rank with the great performances by golfers long past the normal prime years.

Rees, in keeping with his fighting abilities in matchplay golf, was one of the few British players of his times to be truly successful in Ryder Cup play in the face of a general American superiority. He is best remembered as the playing captain of the team which won the trophy at Lindrick in 1957, the first such success since 1933. In all, Rees was playing captain successively from 1955 to 1961 and was non-playing captain in 1967. He played in every match from 1937 to 1961 and was one of the few Ryder Cup team-members who were expected to win their singles matches.

Matchplay, by the time Rees emerged as a leading golfer, had become only a small part of the competitive scene. Happily, he was equally effective in strokeplay events and always regarded as a main hope of Britain producing an Open Championship winner. Having finished in the top dozen twice before the Second World War, Rees had one of his best chances of winning in the first post-war event in 1946 at St Andrews. In the second round he produced the lowest round of the championship, a 67, and went into the final round level with the eventual champion, Sam Snead, and tied for the lead. Alas, he hit his tee shot at the 1st against the rails which run along the right – and went on to take seven on a hole that is in truth quite an easy par 4. No doubt shaken by this, he three-putted the next two greens and that was that. He finished with an 80 and a tie for 4th.

In 1950 at Troon, he was in the lead after 36 holes, tied for the lead after 54 holes and went out in his final round in 33 before dropping two strokes on the 10th and finishing 3rd. He achieved that position once more at Birkdale in 1954 after being tied for the lead after 36

David James Rees (1913–83) Wales, was born in Barry, South Glamorgan. A leading figure in British golf from the late 1930s to the early 1960s.

Dai Rees, delighted at winning the 1957 Ryder Cup match at Lindrick, shakes my hand. Alas, I had just lost my singles to Fred Hawkins

holes. A par at the last would have tied him with Thomson. Rees thought he had hit a perfect 4-iron to the green but his ball skipped through and he took five. Afterwards, Rees noticed a black scorch mark on his ball and considered that it might have landed on a small pebble. Perhaps a more significant detail, however, was that Rees was a nervous starter and only once in this championship managed to par the 1st – not a difficult par 5 at the time.

Dai's last chance came in 1961, again at Birkdale, when he was 48. He was co-leader after the first round and one behind Arnold Palmer going into the final round. Palmer then increased his lead so that only Rees remained in the race near the end and he was four strokes behind with only five to play. He then produced a magnificent finish with birdies at the 15th, 16th and 18th. It wasn't quite enough, though, and Rees was 2nd.

In some ways, Rees was an unorthodox player. In days when even professionals didn't learn a standard method, he gripped the club with all ten fingers on the shaft, one of the few great players of modern times to do so. There is little to be said against this grip, especially for a man with short fingers like Rees. However, towards the top of his backswing, Rees allowed the club to slip into the slot between right thumb and forefinger. This meant he had to regrip on the downswing and may have been the cause of an occasional bad shot.

His early strength was excellent putting, using a slicing action, while the mature Rees was an extremely reliable driver and one of the few British players of his times to master the wedge, imitating the soft knee-action of the Americans.

Rees won six national Opens and had nearly 30 tournament wins in all, mostly in Britain. As late as 1973, at the age of 60, he tied for 2nd place in the Martini Tournament.

ALLAN ROBERTSON

Robertson never won an Open Championship for the simple reason that he never competed in one; the championship hadn't been invented. Rather he was one of the reasons for the championship beginning in 1860. While Robertson lived, there was little doubt that he was the best player in the world. One of the things an Open Championship would do was settle who would be his successor.

Allan was no power player but relied on being long enough and more accurate than his contemporaries. He had a long, relaxed swing

Allan Robertson (1815–59) Scotland, was born at St Andrews, Fife.
The first man to regularly use an iron club for approaching and had a steady all round game.

Allan Robertson was one of the first golfers to have his photograph taken in a studio

and there was no sign of brute force at any point. Some of the clubs he used survive and their lightness is good evidence of this.

In Robertson's day, golf was a game for the few, predominantly played in Scotland, though Scotsmen far from home had formed clubs by this time near Manchester and at Blackheath. I dare say other lone Scotsmen might also have been seen out with a club and a feathery keeping their hand in.

In Scotland golf was not a game for the common man: only two classes could afford to play, the gentry who had enough money to buy clubs and the highly priced balls, and the few who made them. Robertson was one of the foremost craftsmen at this art of his day and, like the rest in the trade, delighted in playing the game after he had closed his workshop on the edge of the Old Course at St Andrews. Old Tom Morris was apprenticed to him and together they made the most formidable foursomes pairing in the land. When the gutta percha ball began to come into use in 1848, Robertson, correctly, feared it would kill his feathery ball trade. He made Old Tom promise not to play with one and burned any he could find. The pair fell out when Old Tom used one of the new balls when he ran out of featheries but it wasn't long before Robertson realised that he had better make rubber balls instead. He quickly adapted his golf to the new ball, especially developing use of the iron instead of the baffy for approaching. This wooden club was short in the shaft and very lofted and used so that turf was taken before the ball.

Robertson is the first man known to have been asked to lay out golf courses and was generally in charge at St Andrews when the course was widened to much its present form. It can be speculated that he designed the most feared hole in golf – the 17th or Road Hole. The year before his death from jaundice, he became the first man to break 80 on the Old Course.

DOUGLAS ROLLAND

One of my 100 greatest, Allan Robertson, played in no championships because they had not yet begun. Doug or Douggie Rolland was a very different kettle of fish. He knew that he was the best and didn't care to exert himself in championships to prove it for posterity. Even so, his competitive achievements were formidable.

After the death of Young Tom Morris in 1875, no great player emerged as his clear successor. In 1883, however, Hoylake decided that they had the best player in Britain in John Ball, and they issued an open challenge. This was taken up by Doug Rolland, who had finished 13th in his first Open in 1882 and 10th in 1883, both times as an amateur. The match was fixed up on a home-and-away basis at Elie and Hoylake, 36 holes each.

The match began at Elie where Rolland finished 9 up. Ball did a lot better at Hoylake but still went down by 11 and 10. With a day to spare and people coming to watch the titans, both men agreed on a rematch. With six holes left to play, Ball was 5 up, but Rolland then won all the remaining holes. He had proved his point.

In 1884, Rolland made his bid for the Open Championship, played at Prestwick. The score-keeping was none too thorough in those days, but we do know that 20 players returned their scores; Jack Simpson won and Rolland tied for 2nd place. Did this cause his ambitions to centre on winning the Open as his chief aim in life – after all, he had played in it three times and was obviously about to win? Well, apparently not. Research among incomplete records would suggest that he played in the Open just once more. This was a full ten years later when the event was played in England for the first time at Sandwich.

What had Douggie been doing in the meantime? Rolland had been a stone-mason, or possibly a builder's labourer, from the age of 13, and he seems to have become a professional golfer at some point between his appearances in the 1883 and 1884 Opens. When he played against Ball, he was probably thought of as an amateur but in 1885 when the first Amateur Championship was held at Hoylake, his entry was turned down. Perhaps the reason for this was that he was a man who worked with his hands and therefore not a gentleman. Douggie next appears on the scene as a professional golfer when he took the job as club professional at the Worcestershire Golf Club, whose club history makes mention of his magnificent play there from 1888 onwards. In due course, Rolland moved on to Limpsfield Chart, Rye, Eastbourne, Bexhill and then became a stoker on the Atlantic run.

In this period, there is no record of his competitive achievements – except in 1894 at Sandwich. Before it, Rolland hammered J.H. Taylor in a challenge match at St Anne's Old Links, supposedly demoralising him with his straight and much longer driving. Then came the Open.

Douglas Stewart Rolland (1860–1915) Scotland, was born at Earlsferry, Elie, Fife. At his peak he was recognised as the best player and his soaring straight driving was a cause for wonder.

Douglas Rolland pictured in the 1890s

Taylor won by five strokes – from Rolland – but Douggie's second round 79 was equalled by only one other competitor throughout the championship. Afterwards, an unusual tournament was played which began with the eight best amateurs facing the same number of professionals. Of the amateurs, Freddie Tait did best. Only two amateurs were left after the encounters in the first round but Tait reached the semi-final, where Rolland disposed of him. Then Rolland had to meet J.H. Taylor who had just been crowned Open champion: Rolland won by 2 and 1. That was certainly the end of his Open Championship career and his name quickly disappeared from any kind of competitive golf.

I can offer a few reasons, more surmises really, for this. After he arrived at The Worcestershire in 1888, it is said that he never again went back to Scotland. There are rumours that there was some trouble with a woman. His behaviour in his first English club job was impeccable and he was much loved – the caddies there even went so far as to mark one green with the words: 'D.R. is a man'. But there are tales of his appearing at exhibition matches without his clubs and bearing the signs of a riotous night. As often as not, he could then go out and break the course record, J.H. Taylor reports. Perhaps that sort of thing cannot last.

After working on the Atlantic run, Rolland lived in America for a while, though apparently he was not involved in golf. He returned to England, his magnificent physique crippled by arthritis or rheumatism, and died at Farnborough as professional to the Aldershot Command Golf Club.

He is easily the most enigmatic of my 100. Who knows what a player he might have been with today's incentives.

GENE SARAZEN

*Eugene Saraceni
(1902–)
USA, was born in Harrison,
New York.
One of the great players of one
of golf's golden ages, the
1920s. He won the Open
Championship in 1932, the
US Open in 1922 and 1932,
the US PGA in 1922, 1923
and 1933 and the Masters in
1935.*

One of very few golfers to change his name, Eugene Saraceni ceased to be so-called at about the age of 17. By then, the young man had decided that he wanted to be a professional golfer and his Italian name was more suited to a violinist or restaurateur.

Walter Hagen, who well knew how to needle a man, used to play on Gene's sensitivities in this matter and in public often used to call him 'Eugene' and also 'Kid'. The latter was a reference to both Sarazen's height (he was five feet five inches tall), and his youth. Sarazen was indeed one of the youngest great champions ever, even beating his exact contemporary Bobby Jones to a first major.

Sarazen, in 1922, was playing in the US Open for only the second time and had only a Southern Open victory to his credit. With a round to play he was not in the heat of contention but got to the turn in 33 in his final round. He dropped a stroke on the 10th but got it back on the 12th. Five pars followed and Gene, on the last tee, needed a par 5 to beat one of the early starters, Bill Mehlhorn. With a couple of driver shots he reached the last green and two-putted. That took care of Mehlhorn and Sarazen's 68 was the lowest final round shot in the US Open. The championship wasn't his yet, however. Sarazen too had been out early and others among the leaders hoped to catch him. One by one they failed, including Jones, who needed 36 home to tie and took one stroke more. Sarazen was champion at the age of 20 years and 4 months. There were many who thought his victory a flash in the pan. After all, it was Bobby Jones who was considered the sure-fire future star. But Sarazen rubbed it in by winning another major championship the same year when he became the youngest PGA champion.

The same event was the scene of one of his finest achievements the following year. Walter Hagen had won the title in 1921 but had not bothered to enter the following year. He was back for 1923, however, and got through to the final; so did Sarazen, who had beaten Hagen in 1922 in a challenge match billed as 'The World Championship' (Hagen had won the British Open). This PGA final was perhaps the greatest in the history of the championship. Sarazen knew, as he later wrote, that 'You couldn't rattle Hagen whatever you did'. This time, however, he succeeded. The pair were still all square after 37 holes. Hagen then hit a good tee shot; Sarazen seemed to have hooked out of bounds. However, his ball was found in play and he hit his second shot almost dead. For once, Hagen seems to have been disconcerted, hitting his approach shot into a bunker. At the age of only 21, Sarazen had three major championships to his credit; it was to be a very long time before he won another.

Sarazen didn't know how to cope with playing badly and as the

reflexes of extreme youth declined, flaws in his playing technique began to play havoc with his game. The main problem was his grip. Neither thumb was down the shaft and he used a form of interlocking grip where the left thumb overlapped the right little finger. In practice he developed blisters – a sure sign that the club was moving in his fingers, probably at the top of his backswing. Sarazen tried an orthodox grip. It didn't work for him; he lost length from the tee and his iron shots lacked bite. He went back to his old grip and worked on strengthening his fingers so that he could hold on securely. He made himself a 30 ounce driver and swung it for an hour a day, in and out of season.

He continued to win tournaments – though for a few years after 1923 he was not successful – but the years went by with no more majors, though he came close a few times. The Open Championship was his main aim but for several entries he performed badly, even failing to qualify in 1923. Even so, it was the event in which he returned to the very top in 1932 at Prince's, Sandwich.

Gene Sazazen, who failed to qualify in the Troon Open Championship of 1923, is seen driving from the 1st tee at Hoylake the following year

Gene: the proud holder of both Open trophies

By this time, Sarazen had cured more than his grip problems. He had also found the answer to sand play. He is credited by many with having invented the sand wedge the previous winter. He wanted a club which would ride through the sand instead of digging down and he soldered lead onto the trailing edge of a pitching club till he got the result he wanted. Suddenly, he was a very good bunker player.

At Sandwich, he led the first round and was never much threatened thereafter. He won by five strokes and his 283 total broke the championship record which wasn't bettered until 1950.

Back in the United States the US Open was scheduled for Fresh Meadows – a course Sarazen knew very well, having been professional there at one time. However, local knowledge doesn't always help and Sarazen was well off the pace after opening rounds of 74 and 76. He was playing too cautiously, knowing he was in the sort of form where he really ought to win. After nine holes of his third round, he was doing no better and decided, rather like Jack Nicklaus in similar situations years later, that he had nothing to lose by going for his shots. Suddenly he began to turn it all around and the strokes began to come back. He finished that round in 70 and then went out again and shot perhaps the finest competitive round of his career, a 66. After 43 holes he had been seven behind the leader and he went on to win by three strokes.

Sarazen, in the long years ahead, never tired of telling this tale, but a much taller story – when what couldn't happen, happened – still lay ahead. In the 1935 Masters (though they were still calling it the Augusta National Invitation Tournament), with four holes to play, Sarazen needed to birdie three of them to tie Craig Wood, who was already in the clubhouse. Preparations for the presentation to Wood went ahead. Journalists concentrated on polishing their reports of how the new champion had done it. With just a handful of spectators watching the pairing of Hagen and Sarazen on the 485-yard 15th, the latter took out his 4-wood, turned the toe in a little and let fly. That second shot found the front edge of the green and skipped on towards the back of the green – and into the hole. It drew him level with Wood and is still the most famous and decisive shot ever played in all the long history of golf. Gene parred the remaining three holes to tie Wood and then won the play-off.

In his career, Sarazen won some 36 titles and this was the last of his seven majors. He continued to compete occasionally year after year, his last significant moment coming at Troon in 1973 when he twice played the short 8th, the Postage Stamp, without using his putter. The first time he punched in a little 5-iron and holed in one; the next day he was bunkered from the tee and holed his next. Quite a way to go out of championship golf.

*Old Tom Morris (rear) and
Allan Robertson study a putt*

ABOVE: *The shot that won Tom Watson the US Open*

RIGHT: *Calvin Peete*

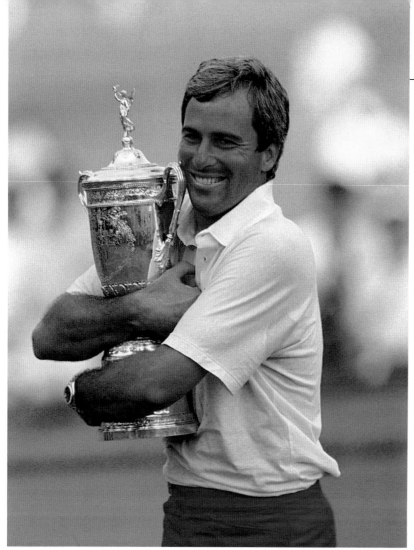

Gene Sarazen always starts off the Masters

OPPOSITE: Jan Stephenson: Australia's most successful woman golfer

BELOW: Sam Snead at the end of another perfect swing

Fuzzy Zoeller plays his tee shot from the 9th at Turnberry

LEFT: *Kathy Whitworth: winner of the most US tournaments*

RIGHT: *Lanny Wadkins holes a good one at the Belfry in 1985*

DENSMORE SHUTE

In Britain during the 1930s – and for quite a long time afterwards – professional golf tournaments always finished on a Friday, including the Open Championship. You might well ask why. After all, the chance of weekend gate money was being thrown away. The reason was that we tournament golfers had a higher calling: we had to be back at our home golf clubs to hand out the Bromfords, Silver Kings and Dunlops to our members.

This state of affairs virtually ended in the United States after the Second World War. In America, the top players were tournament professionals while we remained club professionals who also competed in the relatively few tournaments. During the 1930s, however, nearly all US players were firmly attached to golf clubs and Denny Shute was never a full-time touring professional, but always gave his club first place. No surprise then that he ended his working life as pro with the US golf club that he had been with for more than 20 years. As a result he won far fewer tournaments than he might have but his record in the majors is excellent.

Shute played as an amateur until he was about 24 but soon made his mark as a tournament player when he won the Los Angeles Open two years later. In 1931 he made the US Ryder Cup team – but only just. There was a 72-hole qualifying tournament arranged to decide the last four players. Billy Burke, Whiffy Cox and Craig Wood took the first three places and were in, Shute then won an 18-hole play-off for the last place. The Americans always took winning a Ryder Cup team place seriously, if not the match itself.

Having got himself into the team, Shute made the most of it. In the 36-hole foursomes he and Walter Hagen hammered George Duncan and Arthur Havers by 10 and 9 and in his singles the next day Shute beat Bert Hodson by 8 and 6.

Not surprisingly Hagen used him as one of his strong men at the bottom of the order in the singles for the next Ryder Cup match at Southport and Ainsdale in 1933. It proved to be the last match out on the course with the overall match score level and Shute and his opponent Syd Easterbrook all square on the last tee. Both bunkered their drives. Shute then went for the green but found another bunker. Easterbrook played safely out but well short. In three both were some five yards from the hole. Nearby, US captain Walter Hagen wondered if he should tell Shute to play it safe. If Shute could only get down in two, the match would be tied and the United States, as holders, would retain the cup. The trouble was that Hagen was chatting to the Prince of Wales and it just wouldn't do to walk away.

Shute went for glory but ran about six feet past the hole. Easterbrook's putt wasn't good either but it got perhaps a couple of feet

Herman Densmore Shute (1904–74)
USA, was born in Cleveland, Ohio.
A leading American player throughout the 1930s. He won the Open Championship in 1933 and the US PGA Championship in 1936 and 1937.

Densmore Shute, US PGA champion, drives off at Walton Heath against Henry Cotton (under the umbrella). Cotton had just won his second championship at Carnoustie and won this match, too

closer. To British cheers Shute then missed and to a great roar Easterbrook holed his. It was said of Denny Shute in 1933 (as it was of me in 1953) 'You lost the Ryder Cup'.

But it wasn't long before Shute avenged the honour of the United States. The teams went off to St Andrews for the Open Championship. Shute began with three rounds of 73 and went into the final 18 holes on 219, three strokes behind the leaders who were Henry Cotton, Joe Kirkwood, Abe Mitchell and, yes, Syd Easterbrook. The first three took 79 or worse but Easterbrook looked like a winner again until he had a 7 on his card. Like clockwork, Shute had another 73 to tie with Craig Wood and then win the 36-hole play-off.

Shute reached his first US PGA final in 1931, losing to the unknown Tom Creavy, and won his first in 1936. He finished off his opponent, long-hitting Jimmy Thomson with a 3-wood from the fairway which ended stone dead. The following year, he showed his matchplay quality by winning again. This victory produced a famous challenge match in which Henry Cotton, just crowned Open champion after his 1937 victory at Carnoustie, played Shute as PGA champion for 'The World Championship' and a stake of £500 over 72 holes at Walton Heath. Cotton was at his best and won by 6 and 5.

Shute came close to winning the US Open. He was 4th in 1928, 3rd in 1929, 4th in 1935 and tied with Craig Wood and Byron Nelson in 1939. Nelson won the play-off. Shute was back again in the thick of it in 1941, finishing 2nd to Craig Wood.

As you can see, Shute had a magnificent record but his name is in the record books and not in golf legend; perhaps he lacked spectator appeal.

HORTON SMITH

Towards the end of the 1920s, Bob Harlow began to get a US Tour of sorts organised. He concentrated on the winter months when the professionals weren't busy at their home golf clubs. It was then that the 'Joplin Ghost' first appeared and broke all records. It happened in the winter of 1928/9 and Horton Smith was perhaps the first man to owe his successes to the new steel shafts. Slightly older men than he had, of course, grown up with hickory and it took them time to adapt and make full use of what is still the greatest advance ever made in golf equipment except, some might argue, for the gutta percha ball.

Instead of a long, sweeping swing, Smith emerged with a three-quarter backswing and a pronounced dipping knee action – perhaps

*Horton Smith
(1908–63)
USA, was born in
Springfield, Missouri.
Although a great figure of his
times, he once seemed destined
to be a consistent world-beater.
He won the Masters in 1934
and 1936.*

*Horton Smith drives at the
7th during the Open
Championship at Hoylake in
1930 in which he tied for
fourth place*

the forerunner of the Byron Nelson method which followed some years later. At the age of 20 he won nearly everything on that 1928–9 winter tour. Henry Cotton, in the States to see what he could learn, credited him with winning 11 out of 17 tournaments and being in the top three in all the others. Other authorities credit him with only eight – but what a performance before your 21st birthday. Of course, he was leading money-winner by a mile. Most of the other players were discouraged because Horton, though they didn't care for his short backswing, made the game look so easy: down the middle of the fairway, knock it on to the green and then one or two putts.

He didn't let success go to his head and believed in being early to bed with no smoking or drinking. At one golf club function, he was offered a cigarette, which he refused, and then a drink, with the same result. 'Haven't you got any vices?' he was asked. Horton blushed and looked guilty. 'Yes,' he admitted, 'I sometimes leave my putts short.'

In fact, Smith was recognised as one of the greatest putters of his times. This wasn't much noticed at first because the rest of his game was so remorseless. Then he had an accident, damaging a wrist and being out of the game for some time. He was never quite as good again but his putting, with its beautifully leisurely action, wasn't affected. He was also the first man to use a sand iron in competition, a little before Gene Sarazen is supposed to have invented the club. Horton Smith's came from the Texan, Edwin Kerr McClain. It weighed a massive 23 ounces and had a concave face and was declared illegal by the US Golf Association who ruled the ball was struck twice. Manufacturers then squared it off.

Though Smith was never again quite the man of his first season, he went on to win 30 events in the United States in 1928–41 and, like Old Willie Park, Horace Rawlins and Jim Barnes, his name will always stand at the head of one championship list. Horton Smith won the first Masters of all, in 1934, and repeated his success in 1936.

He was chosen for every Ryder Cup team from 1929 to 1937 and also the teams which didn't play in 1939 and 1941. After suffering Hodgin's disease for several years, he collapsed and died during the 1963 Ryder Cup matches in Atlanta.

MACDONALD SMITH

Bing Crosby was a keen golfer all his adult life and a very good one at that. As an entertainer, he was able to play with all the top players of the 1920s, 1930s and, of course, began his own tournament in the late 1930s. He was once asked who had the best swing he had ever seen. Crosby paused a moment, thoughts of Sam Snead or Bobby Jones perhaps passing through his mind. 'Give me Mac Smith, any day', he said.

Smith was one of three Carnoustie brothers who tried their luck in America. Alex and Willie were the others and he joined them once they were established. Macdonald was then in his late teens. It was obvious that he would be successful and better than either of his brothers, even though both had won the US Open. There was almost conclusive evidence when he came up through the field with a very fine last round 71 to tie for the 1910 US Open with Johnny McDermott and his brother Alex. Macdonald was only a few weeks past his 20th birthday.

Although Macdonald lost his play-off to his brother Alex, he had arrived and it seemed certain that there would soon be another US Open champion in the family. But it didn't happen. Macdonald Smith won numerous tournaments but he couldn't win the two that really counted: the Open Championship and the US Open. Depending on how you look at it, he never got as close as when he was 20 years old.

Crosby wasn't alone in thinking Mac Smith the greatest of swingers. Tommy Armour wrote movingly about Smith in 1935:

> Macdonald Smith is the master artist of golf and the art of golf has denied him national championships. This fickle and irrational art has crowned as its rulers men who are mere caddies compared to him .... He has the cleanest 21-jewel stroke in golf. He treats the grass of a golf course as though it were an altar cloth.... There is luck – plenty of it – in winning national opens.

They say he didn't take a divot in his entire career – hence Armour's 'altar cloth' comment.

Although so good, so young, Mac Smith's play seems to have declined from, roughly speaking, his mid-twenties to early thirties. For a period of his life he suffered from alcoholism and seems to have been saved by a religious conversion. At one stage, he gave up tournament golf and became a shipyard worker, returning to golf around 1923.

Macdonald Smith's troubles in national championships were twofold: often he started with a poor round and when he produced his best stuff over the last 18 it was a case of too little, too late. On other occasions, he might seem poised for victory with a round to play – or even two or three holes – and it would all go wrong.

Macdonald Smith (1890–1949) USA, was born in Carnoustie, Scotland. He had one of the most admired swings in golf history.

Macdonald Smith's balance here isn't perfect – perhaps why he took 82 during this Open in 1925

One of the classic losses of an Open Championship was Smith's defeat at Prestwick in 1925. He played the first three rounds in 76, 69 and 76, which gave him a five-stroke lead. All of Scotland turned out to see a native son win. Crowd control was almost non-existent and Prestwick has never since been used for an Open. When a 78 would have been good enough to win Mac Smith took 82 partly because he was engulfed by the crowd.

In the years 1930–32 he was in contention in all three Open Championships. At Hoylake in 1930 he began with a fine 70 but then fell

CRAIG STADLER

'They're all clones on the US Tour these days': how often you hear that remark, and there's some truth in it. If current players were more colourful, I'm sure the US Seniors' Tour would not be the huge success it has been over the past few years. Many people prefer to watch old-timers like Arnold Palmer, Gary Player, Peter Thomson, Gene Littler and other great names of the 1950s and 1960s than the young players who arrive from the American college golf system.

Yet there are plenty of exceptions. No one has ever called Craig Stadler a clone. Indeed, he would have fitted into the 1930s scene to perfection with his walrus moustache and there might have been more scope for him to express the emotions which so obviously lie close to the surface. As it is, even when Stadler missed a tiny putt on the last green in the 1985 Fourballs, which allowed Sandy Lyle and Bernhard Langer to halve their match at a crucial stage in the contest, he bore that and poor Ryder Cup crowd behaviour with equanimity.

Stadler had a very successful career as an amateur. In 1971 he won the World Junior Championship and the US Amateur Championship in 1973 – the year it returned to matchplay. He beat defending champion Vinny Giles in the semi-finals and romped away with the final by 8 and 6. Stadler turned professional not long after appearing in the 1975 Walker Cup but found it hard going. His temper was by no means always under control. In 1976 he won a paltry $2,702 but began to make a living the following year. In 1978 he won the Magnolia Classic, which has a relatively weak field because the event is held at the same time as the Masters. But a win is still a win and his confidence rose. Stadler became a top US Tour player in 1980 when he won twice and shot up to 8th on the money list, maintaining that position the following year after winning again.

His biggest year was 1982. He started fast, winning the first Tour event, the Tucson Open, then came very close to the Crosby before reaching his goal of winning a major championship. In the Masters, Stadler had a poor start with a 75, improved to a 69 and then took the lead with a 67. The three-stroke lead he took into the final round was a direct result of his very rare feat of having birdies on each of the last three holes. On the final day, he began to leave the field far behind, with a five-stroke lead after 11 holes, but then it all began to go wrong. Stadler had played the last round with Ed Sneed during his collapse in 1979. Perhaps Stadler remembered that disaster. Whatever the reason he dropped strokes on the 12th, 14th and 16th but still came to the last with a par good enough for outright victory. Alas, Stadler three-putted. He had tied with Dan Pohl who had finished strongly with a 67 to Stadler's 73. Soon, all was well. A par was good enough to win him the Masters on the first play-off hole.

Craig Robert Stadler (1953–   ) USA, was born in San Diego, California. A very powerful player, he also has superb touch on and around the greens. He won the Masters in 1982 and the US Amateur in 1973.

*Craig Stadler: definitely not
one of the clones of the US
Tour*

That year, Stadler went on to win twice more and was leading money-winner. Since then, he has not quite gone on to be the giant figure in the game that many expected him to become, but he had consistent years in 1984 and 1985. Only one more US Tour victory has come his way, bringing his total to eight. He has also won the European Masters in 1985, and the 1987 Dunlop Phoenix in Japan.

Stadler has won more than \$2$\frac{1}{2}$ million and, with his very good short game, is a great accumulator of birdies. He played in the US Ryder Cup teams of 1983 and 1985 and was considered to be one of the most dangerous of the Americans.

JAN STEPHENSON

With Laura Baugh, Jan Stephenson is the woman player who has probably made as much money as a result of her sex appeal as her golfing ability. In Jan's case, however, there is no doubt at all that she is a very superior golfer.

Stephenson quickly rose to the top in her own country, winning her state schoolgirls' championship five years in a row from 1964 and then moving on to four junior titles in the next few years. She also won the Australian Junior Championship three times and her state championship twice. In 1973 she turned professional and that year won the Australian LPGA Championship and four other events. So far, so good but at that time, and even more so today, there is little scope for the female tournament player in Australia. If the top male players must travel

Jan Stephenson (1951–   ) Australia, was born in Sydney, New South Wales. The most successful woman golfer yet produced by her country. She won the Peter Jackson Classic in 1981, the LPGA Championship in 1982 and the US Women's Open in 1983.

Jan Stephenson reaches the inverted C finish

205

overseas to become international stars, this is even more the case for women.

In 1974, Stephenson joined the US LPGA Tour and was immediately successful enough to be named Rookie of the Year. She became a double tournament winner in 1976, the year which really brought her to the forefront on the LPGA Tour when she moved up to 8th on the money list.

Jan Stephenson has been one of the most successful money-winners because of her consistency and ability to keep out of serious trouble. In the years 1976–88 she has only once, in 1980, been out of the top 15 earners and was placed in the top five in 1981, 1983 and 1987. Her first major championship came in 1981, the Peter Jackson Classic, but an even more remarkable victory came in the Mary Kay Classic. Her rounds of 65, 69 and 64 gave her an 11-stroke victory and beat the LPGA record for a 54-hole event by two strokes. This is one of the three years in which she won three LPGA tournaments.

Outside the USA, Jan has won the Australian Open twice (1973 and 1977) and in 1985 won the Nichirei Ladies Cup in Japan and the Hennessy French Open. However, unlike her male compatriots, Jan is almost fully committed to the US Tour and is based in Fort Worth, Texas. She has won over $1,700,000 in the USA and 16 tournaments.

Her good looks have helped to bring her many commercial contracts in the USA, Australia and Japan, and she has rejected offers to pose for both *Playboy* and *Penthouse* but has appeared topless in the French magazine *Oui*. Said Jan in one interview: 'If I feel like flaunting it I'm going to'. Some of her fellow players, however, expressed irritation when she appeared reclining on an apparently unmade bed in the LPGA magazine *Fairway*. 'Quasi-pornography', Jane Blalock called the picture.

Jan has produced a golf video which has sold more than 50,000 copies and also an exercise video for those suffering from arthritis. She is also involved in golf course design and is probably the first woman professional in this business.

MARLENE STEWART

Allowing for differences between the play of men and women, Marlene Stewart is surely the greatest golfer that Canada has produced. Her dominance of Canadian golf is incredible. She won her national closed championship from 1951 to 1957 and then again in 1963, and in the last year it was held – 1968. No doubt she would have had even more victories, had the event been held every year during her career.

The Canadian Open Amateur Championship was held more consistently. This she won in 1951, 1954, 1955, 1956, 1958, 1959, 1963, 1968, 1969, 1972 and 1973. She was still good enough to be runner-up as recently as 1982.

No one approaches her record of nine and 11 wins in the two championships and the scores in some of her finals are a measure of her authority. Three times she faced the unfortunate Miss M. Gay and beat her by scores of 9 and 8, 11 and 9 and 8 and 6.

Her appearances overseas were restricted but she had a very good year in the United States in 1956. She won the North and South, a prestigious title, and then went to the final of the US Amateur, where she met JoAnne Gunderson (later Carner) and won by 2 and 1. Ten years later she met the same opponent in the final and this time went down, but not until the 41st hole, making it the longest final there has ever been in this event.

However, her British title came first, as a result of a comfortable victory by 7 and 6 over the Irish player, Philomena Garvey.

Marlene Stewart-Streit, as she was known after her marriage, had other overseas successes, taking the Australian Championship in 1963 and the World Amateur in 1966. Only one other player, Dorothy Campbell, has won the British, US and Canadian titles and no one else has the Australian title on their record also. One can only speculate what a force she might have become on the US LPGA Tour had she turned professional.

Marlene Stewart (later Streit)
(1934–   )
Canada, was born in Cereal, Alberta.
The finest woman golfer Canada has produced. She won the British Ladies' Championship in 1953 and the US Ladies' in 1956.

Marlene Stewart and her beaten opponent after the 1953 British Championship

CURTIS STRANGE

*Curtis Northrup Strange
(1955–   )
USA, was born in Norfolk,
Virginia.
Currently the leading
American player. He won the
US Open in 1988.*

Curtis Strange came into professional golf with an excellent amateur career behind him. Though he didn't take the US Amateur Championship, he won such major titles as the South Eastern, the Western, the North and South and the Eastern, a title previously won by his father in the 1950s. Curtis was also 1974 NCAA champion and represented the United States in the 1974 World Amateur (when he was also College Player of the Year) and the 1975 Walker Cup.

He found professional golf an uphill struggle, and reckoned it took him three years before he could play as well as he had as an amateur. In his first two seasons he can have done no more than cover expenses, but followed with his first tournament win in 1979. In 1980 he became a 'name' player. With two wins he shot up the money list to 3rd place. He was also becoming known for his consistency. In 1982, he set a new money-winning record for a player without a win during the season.

In 1985 he reached the top. With three wins he was the year's leading money-winner and also came within sight of a major championship: the Masters. He began with an 80, which made it seem inevitable that he would be catching a flight home the following day. However, Curtis came back in style with a 65 to be five behind the lead. When he followed up with a 68, he was at the leader's shoulder, one stroke behind Ray Floyd. As he faced his second shot to the 13th in the final round, Strange had moved into a two-stroke lead. Then came disaster. He sent his ball into Rae's Creek, winding across the front of the green and then tried to play his ball which was on the far bank, half in, half out of the water. Well, professionals don't practise water shots much. His ball got out all right but pitched only halfway up the slope and ran back nearly to where it had started. This time he got his ball onto the green and two-putted for a 6. Langer was now within a stroke of him.

When Strange reached the 15th, the par 5 with another carry over water, he was tied for the lead with Langer, who had birdied the hole. In some doubt about which club to choose, he eventually decided on a 4-iron – and didn't hit it hard enough. He cleared the water, but the ball hit the bank and rolled back in. Another 6 and with it went the Masters. However, Strange had three wins during the year, now a very considerable feat on the US Tour, and enough to break Tom Watson's money-winning record with $542,321. He was the US Golf Writers' choice as Player of the Year.

After a quiet 1986, Strange was again back at the top in 1987, this time accumulating $925,941 with three wins, but no majors.

A major did come his way in 1988 though, and in terms of enhanced status it was the best one for an American to win: the US Open at The Country Club. It developed into a tussle with Nick Faldo, holder of the Open Championship: Strange with a fine putting streak and Faldo

OPPOSITE: *Curtis Strange at
The Country Club,
Brookline, where he won the
US Open in 1988*

playing superbly through the green. Strange went into the last day with a one-stroke lead on Faldo, Scott Simpson and Bob Gilder, but bogeys from Strange early on let Faldo into the lead. He continued with par golf as he had in his final round at Muirfield the year before. After a see-sawing contest they came to the last level. After Strange had recovered to some two-and-a-half feet from sand with his third stroke for an almost certain par, Faldo had a putt from pin high on the right fringe to win the championship: his ball just slid by. It meant an 18-hole play-off the next day.

Strange was in the lead after the 3rd but it was still only a single stroke with six holes left to play. However, he finished strongly for a 71 and a comfortable enough win by four strokes.

Strange had won twice before the US Open but had a quiet spell once the championship was in his pocket. He came back right at the end of the season to win the Nabisco Golf Championship which had a purse of $2 million. The victory took Curtis to a new season's record on the US Tour of $1,147,644. He was leading money-winner for the third time in four years.

The US Tour badly needs a superstar and Curtis Strange seems to have been elected. Many Americans would go further and claim that he is the best player in the world. Personally, I would rate him at number three, behind Seve Ballesteros and Sandy Lyle at this time.

LOUISE SUGGS

Louise Suggs was the most brilliant woman player to emerge in the years immediately following the Second World War and one of a handful of professionals who helped to create the LPGA Tour in that period. With Babe Zaharias and Patty Berg she was one of its first stars and described the early tournaments, which one of them was almost certain to win, as being like 'watching three cats fighting over a plate of fish'.

Mae Louise Suggs (1923–)
USA, was born in Atlanta, Georgia.
Her peak career lasted from the late 1940s to the early 1960s. She won the US Ladies' Amateur in 1947, the British Ladies' Open in 1948, the US Women's Open in 1949 and 1952, the Western Open in 1947, 1949 and 1953, the Titleholders Championship in 1946, 1954, 1956 and 1959 and the LPGA Championship in 1957.

Louise Suggs in 1948, the year in which she won the British Ladies' title. She had won the US Ladies' the year before and went on to capture the US Women's Open in 1949 and 1952

She first made her name as an amateur winning the major regional titles of the USA, including the North and South three times, and then went on to take the US Women's Amateur Championship in 1947. In 1948, on crossing the Atlantic, she became one of the ten golfers to take both the British and US Championships. This was just a year after the Babe had become the first American to win.

As an amateur, Louise won two of the majors open to professionals: the 1946 Titleholders and the Western Open in 1947. Miss Sluggs, as Bob Hope nicknamed her, turned professional after she had nothing left to do in the amateur game and quickly won the 1950 US Open. Her performance was phenomenal: she won by 14 strokes and her 291 aggregate set a record for women's golf which she herself broke in a tournament win four years later.

After she had won four pro tournaments, Louise was elected to the LPGA Hall of Fame in 1951. The decision was primarily based on her amateur achievements and she was also the very first member. Her best years as a professional still lay ahead. In 1952, she won six times and had eight victories the following year. She was leading money-winner in 1953 and always in the top few, but just how consistently it isn't possible to say: records are incomplete.

From the early 1960s, her game began to decline, her last victory coming in 1962. Altogether, she won 50 times on the LPGA Tour, a total bettered only by Kathy Whitworth, Mickey Wright and Betsy Rawls. Louise made a habit of making the occasional Tour appearance – sometimes just one a year – and kept that up into the mid-1980s.

With the eventual boom which came to women's golf in the 1970s, she could reflect that the Tour itself might have collapsed in its first years but for the fame of Zaharias, Berg and herself.

J. H. TAYLOR

Like most professionals of his time, J.H. Taylor came into the game because he grew up near a golf course. This was Westward Ho!, home of the Royal North Devon Golf Club. At an early age Taylor began to caddie there and was soon an enthusiastic player, despite being short-sighted. After he left school at the age of 11, he was first a boot boy and then a gardener's boy followed by a spell as a builder's labourer. All the time, however, he was able to play golf, mainly because Westward Ho! was – and is – common land. Eventually, he was offered a job working on the course.

Soon, Taylor had proved the quality of his golf to himself when he beat Horace Hutchinson, twice British Amateur champion, in a challenge match. After he had moved to Burnham and then Winchester as greenkeeper/professional he again improved his standing in the same way, by beating the great Scottish professional Andrew Kirkaldy.

Taylor continued to play his share of challenge matches and in 1893 entered his first Open Championship at Prestwick. In matches before the event started, Taylor found that he could drive straighter than any of the others, putt well enough and was outstanding in the accuracy of his shots to the flag. In the championship itself, he began with a round of 75 to lead by three strokes. Though he fell away to finish in 10th place, that 75 was the lowest round of the event.

It was a different story the following year at Sandwich. Taylor was steadiness itself and came through to win by five strokes and became the first English professional to take the Open. Most notable had been the straightness of his low driving and his brilliance with the mashie in shots to the flag which he hit high or low according to conditions. He was 23 years old and well and truly on his way. His status as the new genius of the age was confirmed the following year when he won at St Andrews, a course he was always to dislike. This time he had a four-stroke margin over Sandy Herd with the next man, Andrew Kirkaldy, another six further away.

This is Taylor's description of the mashie which had brought him so much success, 'It had a short squat head, deep in face, with about the loft of a well set back iron, and had a hickory shaft fitted to it like a young tree'. Taylor had bought it primarily as a bunker club and for chipping. What was revolutionary in his play was using a club with such a short head for shots from as far away as 100 yards. For many, it was too dangerous a club but Taylor had made the technique pay off.

Though J.H., as he was usually known, seemed unbeatable on the big occasions, other young men were on the rise. One of these was Harry Vardon who had yet to make an impression in championship play but who in May 1896 defeated Taylor by 8 and 7 in a 36-hole match at Ganton. Though Taylor had not prepared himself fully for

John Henry Taylor (1871–1963) England, was born at Northam in Devon. Won the Open Championship in 1894, 1895, 1900, 1909 and 1913. He was renowned for straight driving, superb approaching and ability in foul weather.

the contest, he was still shaken by his defeat. Even so, when Open Championship time came round at Muirfield, Taylor expected to win. His 77 in the first round gave him a six-stroke lead over Vardon and he was three ahead with 18 holes to play. Vardon caught him, however, and went on to win the 36-hole play-off.

For a while thereafter, Vardon carried all before him in the tournaments of the day until Taylor returned to form in the 1900 Open at St Andrews. Here he pulled further away from the field every round and ended eight strokes ahead of Vardon in 2nd place and 13 better than the man who finished 3rd – James Braid. These three dominated the championship in the remaining years up to the First World War. Taylor won twice more, in 1909 and 1913, each time by commanding margins. His last victory brought his tally level with Braid and Vardon at five each and at Prestwick in 1914 it looked as though Taylor might make it six when he led Vardon by two strokes going into the final round. On the 4th, however, he had a disastrous 7 to Vardon's 4 and had the grace to write later, 'For the remaining holes I played like a beaten man as indeed I was'. His eventual 2nd place was one of several he had in the event.

Taylor gave some fine performances after the war, finishing 6th in 1922 and 1925 and 5th in 1924, despite being over 50. He consistently represented England against Scotland and played in the first Britain versus America match in 1921. Later he captained the winning Ryder Cup team in 1933. There were few tournaments to play in in Taylor's days but he did win the German Open the second time it was played in 1912 and the French Open in both 1908 and 1909. He was 2nd to Vardon in the US Open in 1900 – the only time he played in the event during his peak years. Surprisingly, he won the Matchplay Championship, second only to the Open in prestige, only once, in 1908.

Taylor made the most of the opportunities that his great prestige as a golfer gave him. After his first championship win, he quickly formed a successful club-making firm, Cann and Taylor. Later he went into partnership with Fred Hawtree designing golf courses. Despite his limited education he proved to be a fluent and sometimes moving writer, producing regular golf columns and eventually the classic *Golf: My Life's Work*. This autobiography was – most unusually – unghosted.

J.H., throughout his life, played an important role in the development of golf organisations and he was in at the beginning of the PGA, the Artisan Golfers' Association and the Public Golf Courses Association. Eventually he retired to a house in his native village of Northam from where he enjoyed what he called 'the best view in all the world'. One of his daughters still lives in that house.

OPPOSITE: *John Henry Taylor pictured at the turn of the century*

PETER THOMSON

Peter William Thomson (1929–   ) Australia, was born in Melbourne, Victoria. Greatest Australian golfer of all time, he won the Open Championship in 1954, 1955, 1956, 1958 and 1965.

During a long career at the top, which lasted from the beginning of the 1950s until the late 1960s, Peter Thomson was a dominant figure in Europe, Australasia and the Far East. His great career record of nearly 60 tournament victories carried just one question mark: he was always said to have 'failed' in the United States. In fact, like his great Commonwealth rival Bobby Locke, he didn't particularly enjoy playing in America, but in relatively brief forays on the US Tour he always made money and did win a Tour event in 1956. However, when Thomson saw the vast sums of money that were to be made on the US Seniors' Tour, he came out of virtual retirement and decided to try his luck. He took some time to acclimatise to competing and playing in the United States but, having done that, he embarked on his triumphant progress towards the end of 1984. The following year, he carried all before him, accomplishing such feats as winning four tournaments out of five consecutively and eclipsing all money-winning records.

How was it that Thomson, in his mid-fifties, could savage the men he had largely failed to cope with when in his twenties and thirties? The answer is that his swing and nerve had lasted well and that his game was suited to the shorter courses that the Seniors play. Thomson was never a long hitter and was therefore not ideally fitted to compete on the kinds of US courses that were used for many events in his prime years. These favoured the long driver and good putter. As there was little trouble for the tee shot with the rough cut low, there was little reward for Thomson's straightness.

He was a master at keeping the ball in play. He was always prepared to sacrifice length in favour of keeping the ball on the fairway and would often use a 3-wood from the tee for that reason. Playing the par 5s and 4s, his tactics were unvarying. He hit his tee shot onto the fairway in a good position to open up the green. He then played his next one on and then tried to avoid three-putting. This approach was most profitable on tight, fast-running courses. Rewards were less when there was little run or punishment for wayward shots.

Thomson first came over to Britain in 1951. His 6th place in the Open showed that he was an up-and-coming man although it was to be a very long time before he did as badly again: in 1952, he finished just a stroke behind the champion, Bobby Locke, and the following year tied 2nd behind Ben Hogan. He had served his apprenticeship and was ready for Birkdale in 1954, the first time that the course hosted the championship. Thomson was close to the leaders throughout and in the final round, after a target had been set, it looked as though he needed a 70 or 71 to win. He reached the turn in 35 but then faltered with relatively poor iron shots yet salvaged his pars with good long approach putts and by holing some difficult shorter ones. He wanted a

4 at the last for his 70 and almost certain victory. His finish showed his cool nerve. Thomson bunkered his second shot and just missed his putt for a 4. He leaned over his ball on one leg and knocked it in back-handed.

His pursuers all failed narrowly and Thomson became the first Australian to win the Open Championship. He went on to make it three in a row with victories at St Andrews and Hoylake. This was the first time that the feat had been accomplished since Bob Ferguson managed it back in 1882. Could he next equal Young Tom Morris with four successive victories? Not quite: St Andrews in 1957 saw

Peter Thomson wins his fourth Open Championship at Lytham in 1958 after a play-off with David Thomas

Bobby Locke's fourth and final win and Peter Thomson, 'of course', was 2nd.

The Australian's victories had all been by fairly narrow margins, proof perhaps that his nerve held up better than many others. This was so in 1958 when three other players who might have won failed to par the last hole at Lytham. Two who didn't fail were Thomson and Welshman David Thomas. There was a 36-hole play-off which Thomson won comfortably in the end.

Thomson was not yet 30 and it seemed that he had no real rivals, with Locke fading from the scene. In fact, the age of Player and Palmer was around the corner and the Australian began to seem like a figure who belonged to the golfing past, though still a young man. In the championships of 1963 and 1964 he did such un-Thomson-like things as finish with a 78 when in hot contention and then rule himself out next year by beginning with a round of 79. Thomson had no taste for the strong-arm approach of the new hero, Arnold Palmer, who was eclipsing him; the precision of Ben Hogan was his ideal. Perhaps even in his own eyes, Thomson was becoming a figure of the past.

In 1965, the championship returned to the scene of his first triumph, Royal Birkdale. The course was fast-running, suited to Thomson's placement skills and feel for how the ball would run. He was all grim-faced determination, a different golfer from the man who had smiled and chatted his way round during his victory years. As the championship reached its closing stages, Tony Lema, the previous year's champion, was his closest rival. The American, however, finished 5, 6 while Thomson perfectly judged the placement and run of his long irons to the last two greens. It was his fifth victory. He had joined Braid, Vardon and Taylor; only Tom Watson was to equal the feat in the years ahead.

WALTER TRAVIS

If you had mentioned the nickname the 'Old Man' around the turn of the century, everyone in golfing circles in the United States would have known who you were talking about – just as Tom Morris was the Grand Old Man of British golf.

Travis, in fact, was probably the oldest golfer in the 100 greatest to take up the game. He seems to have become interested in sport relatively late in life and tried tennis and cycling. But no, he decided, these were sports for young men. How about golf? That, he decided, offered the best prospects of becoming a champion.

Starting in his thirties, Travis could hardly expect to have a lissome swing but he made up for that by being a good thinker about the game. If he couldn't hit the ball a long way, he'd have to make up for that by being very straight. But, he asked himself, what happens when you play a man who is long *and* straight? Travis decided that the answer was to make up for it on and around the greens. A number of players before him, of course, had tried to become outstanding putters, but Travis may have been the first player to practise intensively getting down in two more when he missed a green. Many golfers seemed to think golf was about hitting greens. Getting down in two more if you missed almost savoured of cheating.

In 1898, Travis entered the US Amateur Championship for the first time. He didn't win but, at 36 years old, he at least reached the semi-finals where Findlay Douglas beat him. More work was needed on his game. In 1899, he lost again to Douglas and in 1900 he met the long-hitter once more in the final. The contrast in styles between the two men caused some mirth: at many of the par 4s, Douglas would be playing a pitch with a niblick to the green while Travis still needed his best with a wood. But he was used to that. At the age of 38 he became US Amateur champion and the future beckoned.

Then the Haskell arrived, the first rubber-core ball, but it didn't replace the guttie overnight. Most of the best players scorned it as they thought it was a duffer's ball. A guttie needed to be exactly struck to get height and distance. They contemptuously called the new balls 'Bounding Billies', mainly because, for example, a half-topped shot would still bound along quite a reasonable distance. That just wasn't golf. Travis gave the matter serious thought. The ball had grave disadvantages. The guttie was still a much better ball for the short game; you could strike it more positively. Travis didn't want to lose his advantage in this part of the game for, perhaps, 30 yards more distance from the tee. Travis decided to use a Haskell and his short game suffered. Those first rubber cores would sometimes even bounce out of the cup. Even so, he was the leading strokeplay qualifier and the only thing that stopped his progress in the championship was the

Walter J. Travis
(1862–1927)
USA, was born in Maldon,
Victoria, Australia.
This was the American, long
before Francis Ouimet, who
showed Britain that US golf
was on the rise. He won the
Amateur Championship in
1904 and the US Amateur in
1900, 1901 and 1903.

assassination of President McKinley. The final, which Travis won by 5 and 4, was postponed for a week.

The next year, 1902, Travis tied for 2nd place in the US Open; it was the highest placing obtained by an amateur up to then and not bettered until Ouimet won in 1913. In 1903 he won the US Amateur again. No one has clearly beaten those three wins in four years – though Bobby Jones was later to win five out of seven – much the same striking rate.

In 1901, as US Amateur champion, Travis had made a trip to England and Scotland in a party but had not competed in the Amateur Championship. With the confidence of his US titles behind him, Travis decided to have a go at the 1904 Amateur Championship at Sandwich. Playing in Scotland beforehand his form was poor. In practice at Royal St George's most of his game revived – but not the putting. Without his holing out abilities, Travis had no chance. Then, the day before the championship began, another American in the party suggested that Travis try his putter. He liked it and his form on the greens returned. It was the famous Schenectady model which had a heavy white-metal head and was centre-shafted. With it, Travis beat such leading players as Harold Hilton and Horace Hutchinson and in the final met the longest driver in British golf – Edward Blackwell. The Schenectady won, 4 and 3.

Travis was not popular in Britain. There were no tears of joy at his triumph. The rather grumpy American went home and wrote about how unwelcoming the British had been and the silence that had greeted his success. Was it R and A revenge that the centre-shaft putter was banned in 1911? Probably not, after all, several years had passed since Travis' victory – but Americans thought it was.

Travis went on to design some great golf courses and to edit perhaps the only golf magazine to demand quality writing from its contributors. It was called *The American Golfer* and it folded in the 1930s during the Depression.

OPPOSITE: *Walter Travis demonstrates his putting technique about ten years after his Amateur Championship win*

LEE TREVINO

*Lee Buck Trevino
(1939–   )
USA, was born in Dallas,
Texas.
The most unorthodox and
outgoing of modern
champions. He won the US
Open in 1968 and 1971, the
Open Championship in 1971
and 1972 and the US PGA
in 1974 and 1984.*

*Lee Trevino drives off the
11th at Walton Heath during
the 1981 Ryder Cup. Sam
Torrance, who lost by 5 and
3, watches*

Lee Trevino's is one of the very few rags-to-riches stories in modern golf. After all the average American (male) tournament player of today often begins to play golf because his father is a member of a country club. The lad begins playing and later accepts a college golf scholarship. By the time he turns professional, he's been playing golf for just about as long as anyone could want to.

Trevino's start in the game was very different. He never knew his father and grew up in a shack without electricity or plumbing. His first taste of 'golf' was hitting crab apples with a broom stick and later helping out at a driving range where he began to develop his highly individual golf swing. He left school at 14 and went to work at a driving range full time before spending four years in the US Marines. When he left at 21 he turned professional, as an assistant in El Paso. For years he knew nothing of the outside world of golf, playing pro-ams and money matches locally.

In 1965 he won the Texas State Open, which set him thinking. The next year he qualified to play in the US Open and came 54th which was no disgrace. In 1967 he tried it again, this time finishing 5th with

$6,000 to take home. There seemed to be money in professional golf. He played some more tournaments, made money and decided to try the Tour full time in 1968. He was already 28 years old.

Oak Hill Country Club and the US Open was the scene of his arrival as a name in golf. He played the typical Trevino game, slicing his tee shots onto most of the fairways, not missing many greens (and getting down in two when he did) and holing his fair share of putts. He was two off the lead after two rounds. He went on to be the first competitor to play all four rounds under 70 in the US Open, and won by four strokes. Some thought it was a fluke. This would be the only tournament Trevino would ever win, they said. His golf swing was the reason for this opinion.

Trevino has a strong grip and adopts a wide open slicer's stance. At the top, his clubface is square to the target, making a hook or pull to the left the likely results. Trevino avoids this by driving through with his legs and pulling the clubhead through with his arms. Together with a few other eccentricities in his backswing, it didn't look pretty or effective. But it worked and continued to do so.

In 1970 he was the leading money-winner and his best year followed. He won four times on the US Tour, including the Open after a play-off with Jack Nicklaus and then crossed over to win the Open Championship at Birkdale. In five weeks he won the US, Canadian and British titles. He was named Player of the Year and was an obvious pretender to the Nicklaus throne.

He didn't quite make it although 1972 was another very good year. Trevino was 2nd place money-winner in the US, won three times and retained his Open Championship title after a close struggle with Tony Jacklin and Jack Nicklaus. He kept on winning on the US Tour but Nicklaus won far more often. Even so, the money continued to pour in year after year. From 1968 to 1980 he was seven times in the top 4 money-winners and never had a poor year, despite severe back problems which some said were caused by his being struck by lightning during a tournament, while others thought his swing placed excessive stress on his lower back.

In the early 1980s, Trevino seemed to be drifting out of tournament golf, occupying himself with television work and business deals. In 1984 he made headlines again by winning the US PGA at Shoal Creek, with all rounds in the 60s. He even came close to a successful defence the following year but Hubert Green beat him by two strokes. Trevino is not a regular on the US Tour today, playing fewer than a dozen times a season. His sights are set on the Seniors' Tour for which he becomes eligible in late 1989. Trevino expects to make a huge killing.

On the US Tour he has won 27 times and collected close to 3\frac{1}{2}$ million. He has ten wins overseas and has played on six Ryder Cup teams and was non-playing captain in 1985.

Trevino holes a good one at Cherry Hills where he came close to retaining the US PGA title

HARRY VARDON

*Harry Vardon
(1870–1937)
England, was born at
Grouville in Jersey.
Won the Open
Championship in 1896,
1898, 1899, 1903, 1911 and
1914 and the US Open in
1900. He was revered for the
grace of his swing and accuracy
of his long hitting.*

One reason why the name of Harry Vardon will always have a place in golf history is that the basic grip used by most players is credited to him. However, although he is so often said to have been the inventor of this overlapping grip, he certainly wasn't. Perhaps Scottish amateur Johnny Laidlay was; certainly he was winning championships with this grip before Vardon appeared on the golfing scene. Both J.H. Taylor and James Braid, Vardon's exact contemporaries, also used the same grip. These three great professionals were equally revolutionary, not so much in the way that they gripped the club, as in the fact that they were among the very first players to maintain a firm grip on the club at the top of the backswing where some authorities of the day, such as Harold Hilton, were advising that it should be relaxed.

However, even if Vardon did not invent 'his' grip he was even more revolutionary in that he totally changed concepts of how the golf club should be swung in at least two ways. People had been amazed at how accurately Taylor played – but they did not strive to imitate his shortish backswing, flat-footed action or cut-off follow-through. Perhaps they were a great deal more impressed by the flailing lash of James Braid's swing. Even so, ordinary players realised then that they could not be a Braid, in just the same way that they know today that they haven't the sheer strength of a Greg Norman, Sandy Lyle or Seve Ballesteros. Vardon, on the other hand, made hitting a long ball look effortless; you just swung the club back quite gently, swept it back through the ball and on to a flowing follow-through. It was all done with apparent ease, the body remaining in perfect balance all the way. Vardon was living proof that the golf club should be swung smoothly. Those who used much more obvious effort got no extra distance as a result.

Harry Vardon also changed ideas about the plane of the golf swing. The long, flat so-called St Andrews swing had been the model. Once Vardon began to be closely observed because of his great achievements it was thought, for a while, that he had an ugly swing. The fellow 'lifted' the club back – or so it must have looked in those far-off days – but what Vardon had done was invent the upright swing. He didn't lift the club; he swung it up, instead of round. Of course, no one would have paid Harry Vardon's methods the slightest attention if he hadn't been a winner and he was far more than that: for a while he was virtually invincible.

Vardon first played in the Open Championship in 1893, the year in which J.H. Taylor caused amazement with his first round 75. Vardon attracted no attention with his rounds of 84, 90, 81 and 89 but this was still good enough scoring to have him in the top 25 finishers. Next year, Vardon moved up to 5th place and was then 9th in 1895. All this was not enough to cause much stir. Taylor had arrived at the very top and looked likely to stay there. This changed somewhat when Vardon trounced Taylor in a 36-hole challenge match in the spring of 1896. A number of critics, however, pointed out that the match had been played over Vardon's home course, Ganton, and Taylor had given himself just a few holes in the evening to familiarise himself with the course.

Few speculated on Vardon's chances when the Open came to Muir-field later in the year and many thought his brother Tom a better player. Taylor remained the hot favourite. Soon, however, all eyes were on Sandy Herd who had a remarkable first round of 72. Had such a score ever been achieved before? Taylor's 77 was as good a score as anyone else managed and on the afternoon of that first day he took the lead by following it with a 78. (Herd was on his way out of contention with an 84.) Harry Vardon was six off the pace. On the final morning he made up ground on Taylor with a 78, three strokes better than the champion managed. Taylor, out first in the afternoon, had to set a good target and did so. Only about half a dozen competitors had a realistic chance and one of them was Harry Vardon who needed a 76 to win.

He was followed by a handful of spectators and no recorders for posterity. His scoring was very steady with no bad holes and he came to the last needing a 4 for outright victory. A 4 was possible after a good drive if the player dared to attempt to carry a cross bunker just short of the green. Vardon decided to play short and then got down in three more to tie the champion Taylor. Oddly, there were no strict arrangements for a play-off. Both agreed to play a short tournament nearby the following day and returned to fight it out over 36 holes. Vardon quickly jumped into a three-stroke lead but Taylor kept worrying at him and was level again after 19 holes. Harry's serenity seemed undisturbed and in the end he took the play-off by four.

He now really set about establishing his supremacy, taking two of the next three Open titles. Impressive as this was, Vardon was also nearly unbeatable in the popular challenge matches of the day and the fairly numerous short strokeplay tournaments. He made a good deal of money from these and from endorsements. Then in 1900 he embarked on a long and strenuous tour of the United States, where golf was really taking off, to promote a new golf ball, the Vardon Flyer, a project doomed by the imminent arrival of the Haskell wound ball. Though he called in at the Chicago Golf Club to pick up the US Open title, this was the end of Vardon's greatest years. Some thought that rushing from train to train around the USA had tired him out or that too much competition had dulled his keenness. What is more than a matter of opinion is that he was soon prey to tuberculosis. When winning his fourth championship in 1903, he doubted that he had the strength to finish the event and shortly after entered a sanatorium. The years following were fairly lean until he won his fifth title in 1911 and sixth in 1914, a feat never equalled: truly a Mount Everest of golf.

Harry Vardon portrayed at the end of a drive around 1909. He never finished in an ungainly position

His achievements in the US Open are also worth noting. Vardon played three times. There was the win in 1900. In 1913 he lost a play-off for the title and in 1920, when 50, looked certain to win until a storm blew up over the last few holes and he finished 2nd.

Besides the peerless swing, what were the features of his game? Legend has it that his tee shots were so accurate that his ball would finish in the morning divot holes if he played again that day. Nonsense of course, but J.H. Taylor put it more sensibly in his 1937 broadcast after Vardon's death: 'I say without fear of contradiction that Vardon played fewer shots out of the rough than anyone who has ever swung a golf club. If the test of a player be that he makes fewer bad shots than the remainder then I give Vardon the palm. He hit the ball with the centre of every club with greater frequency than any other player.'

Years later, Henry Cotton wrote in similar terms about Vardon's pureness of strike when the latter was in his late fifties. Cotton would have backed him against anyone else to hit a ball perched high up with the centre of the clubface. Try it! Others noted how Harry Vardon was more likely to finish close to the hole with a long iron or wood than others playing a pitch shot.

Did he have a weakness? Most certainly: he may well have been easily the worst putter of any of my 100 greatest. In his best years, no one thought him good, and he later suffered from what we call the twitch and Harry himself called 'the jumps'. The rest of his short game seems to have been good enough and when putting it was only the short ones which produced that nervous or muscular spasm. His superiority, however, lay in his play through the green – precision combined with length. Harry Vardon must have been the first player who didn't just expect to reach the par 5s in two but also expected to get those second shots close to the hole.

He was professional at South Herts where he lived a few hundred yards away from the course in a modest house with a perfect lawn from about 1903 until his death, when he was a wealthy man. His grave is in Totteridge parish church to which visiting US Ryder Cup teams used to make respectful calls – so perhaps should we.

KEN VENTURI

Kenneth Venturi
(1931–   )
USA, was born in San Francisco, California. There were more downs than ups in his career but he came through in the end. He won the 1964 US Open.

Ken Venturi's first round of golf was a 172, not good but excusable for a 12 year old. He improved rapidly and five years later was losing finalist in the first US Junior Championship. By 1953 he was in the Walker Cup team and won both his matches, in the singles by 9 and 8 against J.C. Wilson. A little later, Byron Nelson, who has helped several leading players develop their game (including Tom Watson) took an interest in him and Venturi benefited greatly. In 1956 he gave possibly the greatest performance yet by an amateur in the Masters. His start was sensational – birdies on the first four holes – and he went on to complete his round in 66. He kept his lead with a 69 and, in worsening weather, a third round of 75 was still good enough to give him a four-stroke lead into the final round.

Venturi didn't play as badly as his score of 80 makes it sound. Few competitors scored well and Venturi held the lead with just two holes to play. Alas, on the 17th he took a bogey 5 to Jack Burke's 3. That did it. He lost by a stroke to a man who had made up nine strokes on the day's round. Never mind, many thought that Ken would win it sooner or later. He turned professional the following year and continued to earn favourable comments. In 19 tournament entries, he only once failed to win money. In 1958, he gave another good Masters performance but Arnold Palmer was just beginning to be Palmer. Venturi finished a couple of strokes behind.

In 1960, it really looked as if Venturi had done it. He was a stroke better than Arnold with two holes left to play. Palmer birdied them both. It was tough luck but the Masters was Venturi's only real stumbling block. He was winning often on the US Tour and had ten victories between 1957 and 1960. Then it all began to go wrong. In 1961 he hurt his back and then, trying subconsciously to protect the injury, changed his swing. What had been elegant and precise was soon jerky and flat. Venturi plunged down the money list to 66th, then 94th. He could only play a tournament if he received a sponsor's invitation.

In 1964 Venturi, who had made so many headlines at Augusta, didn't get a Masters invitation. But his game was on the mend. The once magical iron player began to strike his shots crisply again. He decided to try to pre-qualify for the US Open, which he hadn't played for a few years, and got through this test.

Venturi began with rounds of 72 and 70 at Congressional, respectable but they left him well behind Tommy Jacobs (72, 64) and Arnold Palmer (68, 69). It all changed quickly the final day, the last time 36 holes were played in the US Open. On the first, Venturi's birdie putt hung on the edge of the hole for seconds, and then dropped in. By the turn, he had four more on his card and his 30 equalled the nine holes record for the US Open.

OPPOSITE: *Ken Venturi pictured in 1964, the year of his comeback and his US Open win at Congressional*

The heat was intense, around 100 degrees in the shade. Many in the field were flagging, Venturi more than most, but he was now tied for the lead. Towards the end of that morning round he edged a stroke ahead of Jacobs (Palmer was on his way to a 75) but he began to suffer dehydration. He was shaking and every stride was an effort. He dropped a shot at both the 17th and 18th but was still round in 66, two behind Jacobs into the final afternoon round.

There was some doubt that Venturi would be able to start and there were stories of salt tablets and doctors being summoned. But not many give up when they have a chance of winning the US Open. An hour later he was on the first tee again and it was soon apparent that though his steps might be slow and a doctor was accompanying him, there was little wrong with his game once he reached his ball. He reached the turn in level par which gave him a two-stroke lead as Jacobs's game began to falter. With five holes to play he led by four strokes. But there were still doubts that he could complete the course. On the 18th, he holed a ten-footer for his par and a round of 70. 'My God, I've won the Open', Venturi said. Ray Floyd, tears streaming down his face, picked Venturi's ball from the hole and gave it to him.

It was a fairy tale. Alas, Venturi was not to be back at the top for any length of time. Shortly after, he suffered a nerve disease of the wrists, arms and hands and lost a great deal of feeling. He did win two more tournaments in 1964, played on the 1965 Ryder Cup team and won again in 1966. That was his last victory.

ROBERTO DE VICENZO

Many golfers have started in the game as caddies. Roberto de Vicenzo's origins were even more humble – he began as a caddie's assistant, one whose main duty was to fetch balls from places the caddie himself preferred not to go. The name of the job sums it up well – *lagunero*, 'pond boy'. However, Roberto was soon playing the game and when he was 15 US Ryder Cup star Paul Runyan told him he could make a living as a professional. By 1944 he was doing so, winning the Argentine PGA and Open that year. A few years later, following the tradition of José Jurado who came so close to the 1931 championship at Carnoustie, he made his first Open Championship appearance at Muirfield. Henry Cotton was extremely impressed by his magnificent striking and played with him in practice, wanting to keep an eye on a man he thought might prove to be his main rival. He also attracted the notice of the great golf writer Bernard Darwin who wrote at the time that: 'He gave more aesthetic pleasure than any other man in the field'.

In the 36-hole pre-qualifying event, Cotton took the honours with a pair of 69s but de Vicenzo was close behind with rounds of 72 and 68. It was to be Cotton's year and Roberto finished in a tie for 3rd place. This was the first of many fine performances in the Open Championship but he couldn't win, despite coming over most years. In 1949, he was 3rd again, behind Bobby Locke, and in 1950 moved up a place, again two strokes behind Locke. In 1953, he was on the same mark as Ben Hogan with a round to play but had a 73 to the American's 68. In 1956 he was 3rd once again but looked as if he might run away with the championship in the Centenary Open at St Andrews in 1960. He began with two 67s, easily the best start since Cotton's 67, 65 at Sandwich in 1934. De Vicenzo then began to wobble, however, missing a tiny putt on the 1st green in his third round, eventually taking 75. In the end, it was another 3rd place.

Putting was indeed Roberto's problem. He was never a confident putter and tended to lose heart if he missed a short putt at a crucial point. Vicenzo was always working on his game, however, and in the 1960s made two changes to his game which seem to have made a big difference even though he was by then an old man in golfing terms. An immensely long driver of the ball who played with draw, de Vicenzo was also occasionally prone to a big hook. He changed his left-hand grip so that the club was far less in the fingers and more across the palm. His troublesome putting became more reliable when he changed his stroke and took the wrists out of it. Even so, and despite his tremendous record, at 44 years old he was a figure of the past over, as he said, 'to see old friends' when he came to Hoylake for the 1967 Open Championship. His career had been a great one, with some 30 national titles won and about 130 tournaments in all.

Roberto de Vicenzo (1923–) Argentina, was born in Buenos Aires. The best player to emerge from South America. He won the Open Championship in 1967.

He began with rounds of 70 and 71 to lie a stroke behind Jack Nicklaus, the reigning champion. Few considered his chances at this point. Roberto had contended unsuccessfully too often.

Before he went out to play his third round, Roberto watched Nicklaus and the present US Tour commissioner, Deane Beman, practising on the putting green in front of the clubhouse. He said to them 'How I wish I could putt like you two for just two days'. Roberto then went round in 67 for a two-stroke lead in the championship over Gary Player and three on Jack Nicklaus. There had been no miracles on the greens but a few good ones had gone down and he hadn't missed any very short shots.

There was a great deal of crowd support for Roberto, one of the most lovable figures in golf I have known. He was out with Gary Player, that supreme short game golfer. Strangely, a decisive swing came on the greens. At the 10th, Roberto single-putted for a 3 and Player took three putts. Soon after, he was out of it. Jack Nicklaus wasn't. With birdies at the 7th and 8th, he drew closer to Roberto and in the final hour or so needed his 4s at the long 14th and 16th to make things really tough for de Vicenzo. On the 14th, however, he took 5. 'I feel better', said Roberto, playing just behind.

Even so, Nicklaus put in a grandstand finish with birdies at both the 16th and 18th. Over the long Hoylake finish, de Vicenzo needed par to win and just three good drives would set them up. He did a little better. The 16th, where he had to play a 3-wood second shot over the out-of-bounds practice area finished in the heart of the green and made the championship almost a certainty. He birdied the hole. On the last two holes, superb drives left him a 9-iron distance from the greens and Roberto de Vicenzo became the oldest Open champion since Old Tom Morris, back in 1867. He was 44 years and 93 days old.

Roberto de Vicenzo had competed quite often on the US Tour and had several wins to his credit. He is best known, however, for the one that got away – and on a technicality at that. On his 45th birthday in 1968 he was playing the final round of the Masters. He began by holing an iron shot for an eagle and then birdied the 2nd and 3rd. He birdied four more holes in the round but dropped a shot on the last for a round of 65. Roberto was cross. That last hole had been stupid. He didn't pay enough attention to his score-card. The 65 he signed for was correct but the scores didn't add up to that number. The total was 66. Roberto was not in a play-off with Bob Goalby. Instead, he was 2nd. He failed to notice that his playing partner, Tommy Aaron, had written down '4' for the 17th which Roberto had birdied in 3; it had to stand. The following year, the Masters organisers changed procedures for card checking.

From time to time, Roberto de Vicenzo has announced his retirement but returns to play golf to a high standard. His swing has lasted and in the end he may even rival Sam Snead as the greatest 'old' golfer ever.

LANNY WADKINS

*Jerry Lanston Wadkins
(1949–   )
USA, was born in
Richmond, Virginia.
An attacking player with
great variety of shot. He won
the US PGA in 1977 and the
1970 US Amateur.*

It's often said today that current US Tour players lack colour and play with agonising slowness. Neither is an accusation you could level at Lanny Wadkins. He is one of the quickest players in the game, moving to his ball crisply, setting up, a glance at the target and then he rips it away at the flag. Altogether he is a devastating player when in full flow.

Wadkins came to the professional game with one of the best records in amateur golf of the past 20 years. He played on two Walker Cup teams and in the US World team and won an impressive collection of titles in the USA. These included the Western and Eastern Amateur Championships and the Southern Amateur twice. More importantly, he won the 1970 US Amateur and that same year proved he could compete with professionals by being runner-up in a US Tour event, the Heritage Classic.

Wadkins turned professional towards the end of 1971 and was immediately seen as a future star during his first full season. He was voted Rookie of the Year with record money-winnings for the time, won the Sahara Invitational and was 10th on the Tour money list.

The following year, 1973, he made further progress with two wins and a move up to 5th on the money list. Even so, quite a long 'down' period followed, perhaps partly a result of health problems. He totally disappeared from the limelight in the years 1974–6. He won nothing and 54th on the US money list was his best placing.

In 1977 he was back again, this time with a major championship, the US PGA at Pebble Beach. More publicity, however, went to Gene Littler. At the age of 47 he was in the lead after every round and was five ahead with nine holes to play but then dropped five shots in six holes. Wadkins, on the other hand, who had begun the final day six strokes back had two eagles on the first nine and finished with a birdie 4 on the 18th. It was enough to tie and he went on to win for the first time in four years on the 3rd play-off hole. With another victory in the World Series shortly afterwards, Wadkins ended the year 3rd on the money list. Apart from a good 1979 it was back to almost complete anonymity for four more years; however he did win both the Los Angeles Open and the Tournament Players Championship. In the latter event, he gave one of his finest performances when with strong winds on the last two days at Sawgrass he won by five strokes from Tom Watson. His ability to manipulate the ball was decisive.

From 1982 on, Wadkins has been a consistent achiever; he may have off years but they are still respectable. His best years were 1983 and 1985 when he was 3rd and 2nd on the money list and totalled five wins. His three 1985 wins, money list placing and stroke average earned him the Player of the Year title.

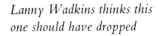

Lanny Wadkins thinks this one should have dropped

In the 1980s, Wadkins has been a key member of the US Ryder Cup team, and has played in the match six times. He has had some success internationally with wins in Japan and Australia. On the US Tour, he has won 18 times and has taken more than $3\frac{1}{2}$ million in money-winnings.

TOM WATSON

Thomas Sturges Watson (1949–)
USA, was born in Kansas City, Missouri.
The successor to Nicklaus as the world's greatest golfer, Watson was eventually overtaken by Ballesteros. He won the Open Championship in 1975, 1977, 1980, 1982 and 1983, the Masters in 1977 and 1981 and the US Open in 1982.

If the Open Championship is also the true world championship of golf (as I believe it has been for nearly 20 years), the competitive greatness of Tom Watson stands out for all to see. In nine years, he won the Open five times. This can be compared with Jack Nicklaus's three wins from 1962 and Seve Ballesteros's three since his first appearance in 1975 at Carnoustie.

Tom Watson in play at Olympic in 1987. He finished second in this US Open

Those championships came to Watson in quite a variety of ways. In 1975 he was unheralded, having thrown away chances in US major championships. With most eyes on such players as Jack Newton, Jack Nicklaus, Johnny Miller and Bobby Cole, Watson suddenly holed a vital birdie putt to set the target. It proved enough for him to first tie Newton and then win the 18-hole play-off. This win must have given Watson an enormous boost for, after a quiet 1976, he became the dominant player on the US Tour which, in those quite recent days, also meant best in the world.

His next Open contained perhaps the greatest example of a matchplay competition lasting two whole days in a major championship. Watson and Nicklaus both began with rounds of 68 and 70 which meant that they were paired for the third round. Again, they finished equal. This time, their 65s outdistanced the field; only Ben Crenshaw was as close as three strokes behind. On the final day, Crenshaw quickly faded out and the stage was left to Watson and Nicklaus, who rapidly went into a three-stroke lead after four holes but Watson came back fast. After eight holes he was level, though Nicklaus was again one ahead at the turn. So it remained for several holes, the pair playing shot for shot. The 15th, a par 3, was a turning point: as Nicklaus contemplated his birdie putt, Watson putted in from perhaps 20 yards away. Lucky, yes, but the shot was perfectly weighted.

He was in the lead for the first time after the 17th, a par 5 in easy range in two. Nicklaus hit his second shot short and then failed to get down in two more. Watson's 4 was always safe. He led for the first time that day – and at the right time. Both birdied the last, Watson's as perfect a 3 as you could wish for – a 2-iron far down the fairway and a short iron more or less stone dead. Before he holed it, he had to watch Nicklaus hole a vast putt for his own 3. But Tom was champion again.

Tom's victory at Muirfield three years later in 1980 was as fine in so far as his scoring almost equalled his Turnberry performance. But there was no head-to-head duel. His third round 64 had discouraged the rest of the field and he won by four strokes.

Troon in 1982 saw a championship which Tom himself said 'was given to me. I didn't win it.' Even so, it's his name on the trophy, not Bobby Clampett's or Nick Price's. Tom Watson was the man who managed a steady finish.

Birkdale in 1983 saw a more classic Watson performance. The course was playing relatively easily, rather as it had been for his Carnoustie victory. As a result, more players than usual got themselves into contending positions. Even so, only Tom Watson and Andy Bean managed every round in 70 or better. Although he held the lead into the final round, nine other players were four strokes or fewer behind. Watson lost his lead, only getting ahead with a birdie on the 16th. He came to the last, a long par 4, needing a par to win – and he had just hit a very poor tee shot to the 17th. This time there was no such error. His drive was long and in the centre of the fairway. His 2-iron, with the crowd swarming around him as he walked to his ball, made nothing of the 213 yards and was struck with a slight draw to hold it into the wind: a superb shot if ever there was one.

If Tom Watson had proved to be an Open Championship specialist, he was equally effective on the US Tour. He joined it in 1971, having caused no great stir in amateur golf, and moved up the money list gradually. In 1974, he won the prestigious Western Open, once a major championship. By 1977, he was the dominant player, the favourite every time he teed up. He was leading money-winner four years in a row, something even Nicklaus hadn't quite managed. His best year was 1980, when he had six victories (by contrast, Curtis Strange has never bettered four).

After this, his pace slackened a little though he was leading money-winner again in 1984, the year in which he suffered what some have seen as a major trauma. In the closest contention with Ballesteros for the Open Championship at St Andrews, he hit an ideal tee shot to the perilous 17th – very close to the out of bounds along the right. Then he put his second shot on the road and that was that. A record–equalling sixth Open was gone, perhaps for ever.

The following year, Watson's game went to pieces. He had no wins and fell to 18th on the US Tour money list. His problem wasn't wayward long shots – he'd always hit a few of those. Watson had been the best in the business at getting down in two when he missed a green; suddenly he could no longer do it. The main problem was his putting. At his peak, he had been almost infallible from close range and had always given himself a chance from longer distances. Seldom did he come up short. He went for the hole knowing he could get the four-footers back. Nowadays, however, Tom is a great deal less sure. He misses his share of short ones and doesn't get the long ones running boldly at the hole yet he remains a formidable player, better through the green than in his most successful years.

Watson has won 32 tournaments including three majors in the United States: the Masters in 1977 and 1981 and the US Open in 1982. Each time, by coincidence, he had Jack Nicklaus hot on his heels. The most dramatic occasion, because it contained one of those obviously decisive shots close to the end, was the Pebble Beach Open. With two holes to play, Watson needed a par 3 and a par 5 to tie. He missed the green with his tee shot on the first of these and was left with a little shot from semi-rough at the edge of the green which was sloping away. It looked impossible to stop the ball close to the hole. To his caddie, Watson said, 'I'm going to hole it'. And he did.

TOM WEISKOPF

Early in 1989 and at the age of 46, Tom Weiskopf announced his increased participation in tournaments during the season. This might have been a sign that he was preparing himself for some lucrative years on the Seniors' Tour when he reaches the age of 50, or that he feels he can still prove something in mainstream golf.

Weiskopf, in fact, is one of those players who I think has not quite fulfilled a magnificent potential. Others may have made the most of quite meagre talents; Weiskopf was a star but not quite the superstar his magnificent gifts promised. Even so, his achievements on the US Tour are formidable. From 1966 to 1982 he always finished in the top 60 money-winners. No one in the game could match such a long stretch as 17 years and illustrates his consistency, something one might not fully expect from a man renowned for displays of temperament and occasional playing disasters.

For most of these years, Weiskopf was very much more than just a top 60 man. In 1968, 1973 and 1975 he finished in the top three and had a run from 1968 to 1978 when he was always in the top 20 and usually came a lot higher than that. He came into professional golf in 1964. His first event was the Western Open which was appropriate because he had won the Western Amateur the previous year. After poor results early on, Tom considered giving up. A little later his performances began to improve, but in 1966 he suffered a duodenal ulcer – probably as a consequence of the strain he felt in tournament golf.

He really arrived as a player to be reckoned with in 1968. He won twice and by the end of the year was recognised as a leading player, coming 3rd in the US money list. Victories didn't come thick and fast, however, and an overseas performance seemed to stir him on to greater achievement. This came in the World Matchplay Championship at Wentworth in 1972, which Weiskopf won, immediately earning a considerable following in England where his on course behaviour was always impeccable and the majesty of his golf swing almost revered.

His greatest year followed. In 1973 he won four times on the US Tour and overseas won the Open Championship at Troon. Sadly this was to be his only major, but it was done with much style. On his arrival, he had won three US Tour events and went into the US Open as favourite. Weiskopf, like a few others, was thwarted by a final round 63 from Johnny Miller and finished 3rd. At Troon, a few weeks later, he began with birdies at three of the first five holes and never looked back. His 68 gave him the lead which he increased to three strokes after 36 holes with a 67.

For the third day he was paired with his main rival, Johnny Miller who quickly caught him and then moved ahead. He was 32 to the turn,

Thomas Daniel Weiskopf (1942–) USA, was born in Massillon, Ohio.
He had one of the most majestic of golf swings but failed to fulfil his potential. He won the Open Championship in 1973.

Tom Weiskopf, whose greatest victory was in the Troon Open of 1973

Weiskopf 37. It was at this point Weiskopf showed the steely resolve so often thought lacking in his make-up. He bettered Miller's score on the homeward nine by three strokes and had regained the championship lead – by one stroke – at the end of the day.

After the 3rd hole on the final day, Tom was three strokes ahead and kept that margin to the end. His total of 276 tied the record set by Palmer at Troon in 1962 and was his fifth win in eight starts. The world was at his feet. There was also a great deal of speculation that Weiskopf had been steadied by the death of his father shortly before, feeling that he really ought to make the best use of his magnificent talents. At Troon, he certainly had. A bad shot was followed by a steady recovery, not a show of hot temper. He didn't three-putt once and gave a great over-all champion's performance (he was the last man, incidentally, to win with the small 1.62 inch ball).

Weiskopf never quite reached these heights again though he continued to win on the US Tour and occasionally overseas. He also came close to taking other majors. By what seems to be the end of the peak of his career he had five times finished in the top four in the US Open with 2nd in 1976 his best finish. In the Masters, he did even better, being 2nd in 1969, 1972, 1974 and 1975, this last year the greatest three-way contest in the history of the event and won by Nicklaus with Johnny Miller and Tom a stroke behind.

At one time 4th in the all-time money-winners' list, Weiskopf took over $2 million on the US Tour and won 15 times. He also had six overseas victories. He appeared in two US Ryder Cup teams and declined a place on another because he preferred hunting in the autumn – a sport he preferred to golf.

He now works in golf television and is earning a considerable reputation in golf course architecture.

JOYCE WETHERED

It may be difficult to compare the differences between the way men and women play the game of golf. Yet, when talking about Joyce Wethered, Bobby Jones had no difficulty at all. He simply thought she was the best player – of either sex – he had ever seen. After one exhibition match with her he remarked that he had never felt so outclassed. This was no freak opinion. Henry Cotton, who played with her more than once, assessed her game: he thought she drove the ball as far as a good male club player and that her fairway woods were as straight as a professional using the pitching clubs. Both her chipping and putting were precise and for overall straightness through the bag, only Harry Vardon could be considered her equal. Although Jones never said an unkind word about anybody, Henry Cotton most certainly did – and quite often. If we take the two views together it is obvious that in Joyce Wethered we have a remarkable golfer.

Her record bears this out in full. She first attracted attention in the 1920 English Ladies' Championship at Sheringham. Joyce had grown up playing with her brother Roger, who won the British Amateur Championship. Sheringham was her first entry in an event of importance, yet she only went for fun and to keep another competitor company. At the time, Joyce Wethered probably had little idea how good she was. Her friend was knocked out early but Joyce was still there as round succeeded round. Eventually, she was in the final, where she was given little chance; she faced Cecil Leitch, the greatest woman player of the day. It all went predictably enough. Miss Leitch was 4 up at lunch, then won the next two holes, and the outcome of the competition seemed to be settled. Then Joyce Wethered produced 3 after 3, was in the lead with four to play and won by 2 and 1. She had arrived. The match with Cecil Leitch was the nearest she ever came to defeat in the English Championship. She won the event every year between 1920 and 1924 which, although most of her matches were over the 18-hole sprint when anything can happen, meant winning 33 consecutive games. She thought that was enough and never competed in the championship again.

She was nearly as dominant in the British Ladies' Championship, though she did lose a couple of matches. In 1921 she reached the final but lost to Cecil Leitch by 4 and 3. In the same year, she also lost the French Championship to Leitch so we cannot say of her, like Bobby Jones, that no one ever beat her twice at matchplay. The 1922 final, however, was a very different story. It featured the same two players; Joyce Wethered romped home by 9 and 7. The next year, she suffered her second and last defeat in this championship when she went out at the semi-final stage. She took the title the following two years, again beating Cecil Leitch in the 1925 final.

Lady Heathcoat-Amory (1901–)
England, was born in London. She was renowned for the all-round excellence of her game. She won the British Ladies' Championship in 1922, 1924, 1925 and 1929.

Joyce Wethered in play at Troon in 1925 for the British Ladies'. In the final she beat Cecil Leitch on the 37th

That, she decided, was enough. Apparently, she much preferred playing golf for fun and had won as many championships as she cared to. In 1929, however, the British Ladies' Championship was scheduled for St Andrews and Joyce thought it might be fun to play there. It was a decision that greatly enhanced her legendary status. The great

American Glenna Collett wanted to add this title to her array of American championships and, like a good film script, the two best players in the world got through to the final. The standard of play lived up to the high hopes. Glenna Collett was 5 up after the first nine holes but lost three of that lead by the end of the first 18. Then it was Joyce Wethered's turn to dominate. She went to 4 up, was pulled back briefly but went on to win by 3 and 1. That made 36 wins from 38 matches in the British Ladies' Championship.

She played no more championship golf. Instead, her talents were mainly displayed in the Worplesdon Mixed Foursomes. She won this sociable event eight times, with seven different male partners, not all of them of quite the highest class. Was this a show of arrogance on her part? After all, she did prove that she could win playing with just about anybody. People could draw their own conclusions.

With the riches to be gained today in the United States and, to some extent, Europe, Joyce Wethered, who was not well off, would surely have turned professional for she forfeited her amateur status in the mid-1930s in order to play an exhibition tour in the United States. Babe Zaharias (then Didrikson) played in some of the fourball matches. Zaharias outdrove Joyce but was outplayed in all other respects. The playing record and career of Joyce Wethered are quite similar to those of Bobby Jones: both won everything worth winning and retired young.

KATHY WHITWORTH

Kathrynne Ann Whitworth (1939–)
USA, was born in Monahans, Texas.
Won the Titleholders Championship in 1965 and 1966, the Western Open in 1967 and the LPGA Championship in 1967 and 1971.

There are two parallels with Sam Snead in the career of Kathy Whitworth: neither player won the US Open (even though the women's version often falls to little-known players) and both were prolific winners of US tournaments. Kathy Whitworth, in fact, is the most prolific of them all. In 1982 she first caught, and then surpassed, Mickey Wright's record of 82 wins. That left Mr Snead to be dealt with. She passed his total in 1984 with her 85th victory and went on to take what may well be her final tally to 88 in 1985.

Kathy Whitworth has won more titles than anyone else in US Tour golf

Her money-winning achievements are just as impressive and include being leading money-winner every year except one in the period 1965 to 1973. Though the career target of $1 million has now become commonplace, Kathy Whitworth was the very first player to get there, in 1981.

Kathy Whitworth had only a couple of state titles on her record when she turned professional in 1958 and it was 1962 before she won her first event. Soon, however, she was challenging Mickey Wright as the most successful woman player ever. In 1963 she won eight events and did so again in 1965. Even more successful seasons lay ahead: she won nine in 1966 and ten in 1968. With the rising standards of women's golf, her victories became less frequent but she had at least one win every year up to 1978.

Her main strength, using a flat, unfluid swing, is that she nearly always succeeds in keeping the ball in play and was the best putter around during her finest years. In an exceptionally long career at the top, consistency was her prime attribute and she still competes regularly on the US LPGA Tour.

CRAIG WOOD

Craig Ralph Wood
(1901–68)
USA, was born at Lake
Placid, New York.
The man who was always
pipped at the post, he
eventually came through to
win major championships. He
won the Masters in 1941 and
the US Open in 1941.

Craig Wood always seemed doomed to finish runner-up. It happened in the 1933 Open Championship at St Andrews for instance. During the final round, he hit one of the longest drives ever recorded (about 430 yards), on the 5th. Little good it did him, for he was bunkered and eventually finished in a tie with Denny Shute. Another vast hit at the beginning of the 36-hole play-off was also wasted. Wood drove his first tee shot into the Swilcan Burn, some 350 yards away but, in the end, he lost by five strokes.

A couple of years later he was the victim of the 4-wood shot that became famous around the world and is still spoken of today. At the very moment when Gene Sarazen holed his second shot on the par 5 15th hole at Augusta National, Craig Wood was apparently home and dry and receiving congratulations on his victory. However, by that one shot, Sarazen made up the three strokes he needed to catch Wood and went on to beat him in the play-off. Such is golf, and similar body blows were suffered by Greg Norman in 1986 and 1987.

In another major championship, the 1939 US Open, Wood, Byron Nelson and Denny Shute tied with 284. Craig needed a birdie on the last hole to win, but another freak shot was to ruin his chances. The play-off was a close fight between Nelson and Wood – Shute was never really in it. The two got to the turn in 33 and the championship seemed to be Wood's when he went ahead for the first time at the 17th, which Nelson three-putted while Wood birdied. At the last hole, a par 5, Wood pulled his second shot into the crowd but seemed to have compensated for the mistake with a superb pitch to about four feet. Nelson sent his third shot to eight feet and made the putt. Wood still had his shorter one to win the championship but just failed. The two tied with 68s and came back the following day. Nelson then almost made sure of the title on the 3rd and 4th. He birdied the first of these and then holed out his second shot on the next with a 1-iron. Craig couldn't close the gap and lost with a 73 to Nelson's 70.

It wasn't until Wood was 40 years old that his luck changed in a big way. He began the Masters that year with a 66 and was still in the lead after three rounds. One of his pursuers was Byron Nelson who then went to the turn in 33 while Wood took 38. However, Wood played the better golf on the homeward nine when his 34 was good enough for a three-stroke victory. A long delayed win in the US Open followed just a couple of months later. Wood was suffering back problems at the time and had to play in a brace. At the Colonial Country Club in Fort Worth, Texas, he began with a 7 on the 1st, a par 5. As he was in great discomfort anyway, Wood began to consider walking in but Tommy Armour managed to talk him out of it. Wood completed the round in 73, a good score that day in poor weather. What won him

the championship, however, were two rounds of 70 on the final day which brought him in three strokes ahead of Denny Shute.

Wood, so long thwarted by bad luck, had won two major championships in a couple of months. Even in this US Open he may have been close to disqualification. During a thunderstorm in the first round, play was suspended by a siren. When Tommy Armour and Wood reached the 8th hole, a telephone was ringing. Armour picked it up. 'You may resume play', a voice announced. For about four holes they had been the only players on the course; they hadn't heard the siren.

Having reached the summit late in his golfing life, Craig Wood did little else of note and achieved his last win in 1944. Besides persistent back trouble, he was finished off by a putting twitch. He served as professional at Winged Foot for a good many years.

My father thought highly of his abilities but still managed to beat him by one hole in the 1935 Ryder Cup at Ridgewood, New Jersey, the only British win in the singles.

IAN WOOSNAM

Ian Woosnam
(1958–)
Wales, was born in
Oswestry, Shropshire.
At the end of the 1987 season
he was acclaimed the best
player in the world.

Although Ian Woosnam went into 1987 as one of the stars of the European game, he had actually won only four tournaments on the European Tour in the years 1982 to 1986, and two on the African Safari circuit. In the years 1982 to 1986 he had always been a substantial money-winner, his placings ranging between 4th and 9th.

Even greater things lay ahead in 1987. The year began with a win in the Hong Kong Open and then Ian made a great start in Europe with wins in the Jersey Open in April, a lost play-off to Seve Ballesteros at the Suze Open at the Mougins Golf Club in Cannes and then his second win in three weeks, the Madrid Open. After making no headlines in May, Woosnam had a stirring battle with Mark McNulty in the Dunhill British Masters at Woburn in early June before losing by just one stroke. But he was back at the top of the money list. In the middle of the month he tied for 2nd in the Belgian Open and tied for 3rd in the Irish Open in early July.

His most dominant performance came shortly after in the Bell's Scottish Open Championship at Gleneagles. His rounds of 65, 65, 66 and 68 meant that he was in the lead all the way and was seven strokes ahead at the finish. Woosnam was the most favoured British player for the Open Championship the following week and did, in fact, produce four steady rounds and tied for 8th place, five strokes behind Nick Faldo.

Woosnam's great money-winning feats came towards the end of the season. His fourth victory was at St Nom-la-Bretêche, Paris, in the Lancôme Trophy. He was 24 under par, winning by two strokes. A month later he became the first British player ever to win the World Matchplay title. In doing so, he beat each of his main rivals for European supremacy in succession – Nick Faldo, Seve Ballesteros and, in the final, Sandy Lyle. In each case the struggles were extremely close, going to the last green before Woosnam won by one hole each time.

However, perhaps the most amazing result came in the World Cup at Kapalua, Hawaii. In this two-man team competition it is obviously essential for a country to field two strong players but Wales had only one: Ian Woosnam. His partner David Llewellyn had won a minor event, the Vernon's Open at Hoylake, but had also missed seven cuts in a nine week spell during the year and finished outside the top 50 on the money list. During the event Llewellyn managed to perform most creditably, averaging in the mid 70s, while Woosnam played brilliantly enough to lead the field individually by five strokes (from Sandy Lyle) with the Japanese Koichi Suzuki another four strokes away. The pair won for Wales in a play-off with Scotland.

On the European Tour, Woosnam had doubled his career money-winnings in a single season, his £439,075 being a new record. There

was more money to come in the Sun City $1 Million Invitation Challenge, which he won, taking his haul to over £1 million for the season. It was his eighth victory.

Despite all that was said and written at the time, I don't honestly believe that 1987 made Woosnam the best player in the world. He has no major championship wins on his record and I would nowadays demand that a player show his worth in the United States. Ian has done nothing of note there to date, except for an excellent performance in the 1987 Ryder Cup matches at Muirfield Village, Ohio.

Woosnam's 1987 left him with the problem of what to do for an encore. Winning is becoming harder in Europe all the time. The year opened with much talk of loss of form when he signed a contract to use Japanese clubs, and some poor performances certainly followed. When he did win again, however, it was a good one: the PGA Championship at Wentworth. He closed with a 67 to win by two from Seve Ballesteros and Mark James. Possibly an even better performance followed three months later in the Irish Open at Portmarnock where his 278 total brought him home seven strokes ahead of Nick Faldo, José-Maria Olazabal and Des Smyth.

Sunningdale Old is perhaps a little short to withstand the modern tournament player and the first five home in the European Open all averaged below 67, a round of 65 being commonplace. However, a 66 was Ian's *worst* round and he won by three from Nick Faldo with rounds of 65, 66, 64, 65.

Woosnam finished the year in 4th place on the money list with some $234,000, behind Olazabal, Faldo and Ballesteros who had beaten his 1987 record with £451,000.

The British like a 'gritty little 'un' and the five foot four inch Welshman rates ahead of both Lyle and Faldo in public affection. A Woosnam Open Championship victory would be enormously popular, and it is something he may well achieve, but I must still rate him behind Lyle and Faldo at the moment. They have won majors and performed in the United States. He has yet to do so.

MICKEY WRIGHT

*Mary Kathryn Wright
(1935–   )
USA, was born in San
Diego, California.
Won the US Women's Open
in 1958, 1959, 1961 and
1964, the LPGA
Championship in 1958,
1960, 1961 and 1963, the
Titleholders Championship
in 1961 and 1962 and the
Western Open in 1962, 1963
and 1966.*

Mickey Wright had a short amateur career. She won the US Junior Championship in 1952 and played her only full year of amateur golf in 1954 where she won the World and All-American titles but was beaten in the final of the US Amateur.

As a professional, she was the leading player by 1958 and reached a peak in the period 1961–4 when she totalled 44 tournament victories. During this spell she set records for both the most victories in one season (13) and the second best (11) which still stand. Mickey Wright

*In 1960 Mickey Wright was
at the peak of her career*

went a stage further than Babe Zaharias in scoring; the latter averaged something like 75 a round, while when Wright arrived winners of the Vare Trophy were producing 74s. Mickey Wright was going round in about $72\frac{1}{2}$ in 1964, her best year.

Although Kathy Whitworth's 88 wins is the record, Mickey Wright won her competitions in a much shorter time span – 81 between 1956 and 1969 with a final win in 1973. After her spate of victories of the early 1960s, Mickey Wright lost some of her interest in competing and went back to college. She had some health problems; she suffered from an arthritic wrist and was later to react badly to the sun. She also developed a dislike of flying, but it was probably a persistent problem with her feet that was responsible for bringing her career to an end.

Though Mickey had virtually none of the charismatic appeal of Babe Zaharias, her dominance of women's golf was even greater. Her deeds raised interest in the LPGA Tour just as the appearance of Nancy Lopez did when she burst onto the scene in 1978. As Mickey Wright was never at the ready with a quote and preferred to be out of the public eye, golf writers had to concentrate on the way she played the game. They thought that her swing was perfection and that no one approached her crisp hand action in hitting the long irons. They also noticed that there were other good women players. Sponsors' interest in the LPGA Tour grew.

Although Mickey Wright has a low profile in golfing legend, mainly because of her reticence, she may be the greatest female golfer ever and she can claim to be the most dominant player in the history of women's professional golf in the United States.

BABE ZAHARIAS

*Mildred Ella Zaharias (née Didrikson)
(1914–56)
USA, was born in Port Arthur, Texas.
Won the US Women's Amateur in 1946, the British Ladies' Championship in 1947 and the US Women's Open in 1948, 1950 and 1954. She also won four Western Opens and the Titleholders Championship three times, events recognised by the LPGA as major championships.*

A triumphant Zaharias with the cup

Babe Zaharias is a key figure in the evolution of women's golf. If Cecil Leitch was the player who showed some 80 years ago that a woman could play with punch, the Babe was living proof that she could also hit the golf ball a very long way. Zaharias did this without the benefit of a massive physique. The Babe was a long hitter because she was one of the most gifted athletes of either sex in history. Though her nickname derives from Babe Ruth – she once hit five home runs in a baseball game – it was her performance in the 1932 Los Angeles Olympics that made her world famous. She won the javelin, the 80 metres hurdles and was disqualified, having set a world record, in the high jump for using the Western Roll, considered unladylike.

The Babe could do just about anything. Earlier, she had been an All-American at basketball while her most fabled achievement came just before the Olympics. In the US national championships she entered eight events and won six of them, setting four world records in the process. It was like the decathlon, only worse: these achievements were crammed into just two-and-a-half hours. And she won the club championship single-handed.

Coming from a poor background, the Babe had to make money from sport. She tried professional baseball and basketball and then gave her full attention to tennis. She abandoned that when she found out that she was not acceptable as an amateur. She had first tried golf during the Olympics when sports writer, Grantland Rice, persuaded her to try hitting a golf ball. All were amazed at the distance she achieved, although it was not surprising from a javelin champion: the Babe had that snap from the right shoulder, elbow and wrist that many women golfers lack.

Even so, when the Babe gave her full attention to golf, she found it did not yield its secrets easily. One problem was that she was treated as a freak on exhibition tours: the interest was in seeing how far she could belt a golf ball. On one such tour, Joyce Wethered showed that there was a great deal more to golf than length. The Babe outhit her, but Wethered outscored Zaharias. Also, dare I say it, golf is a great deal more complicated than perhaps any other athletic pursuit. The Babe, as she put it most picturesquely, 'got fouled up in the mechanics of the golf swing'. She had also to learn over the years to play all those shots in the game which call for touch and artistry rather than the athleticism of the full swing. It all took much more time than setting athletics records and winning gold medals, but she came through. As an amateur, she was barred after winning the 1935 Texas Amateur because she had played other sports professionally (which would be no problem today). Eventually, however, she gained another source of income when she married wrestler George Zaharias, billed as 'the Weeping Greek from

Cripple Creek'. Her amateur golf status was restored in 1943. With the war over, she won 17 consecutive tournaments in 1946/7. The most important were the US Amateur, which she rounded off with an 11 and 9 final and then went on to become the first American to win the British Ladies' Championship. In the six rounds, she lost only four holes!

It was time to try to get professional women's golf on the move in the USA. She was, of course, the great attraction in the new LPGA and in her eight-year career won 31 of the scheduled 128 events. In 1950, she won six out of nine and seven of the 14 the following year, Patty Berg, Betsy Rawls and Louise Suggs providing some of the very strong opposition. That same year, she visited Britain with a US women's team. In a match against a select team of London amateurs she played former English champion Leonard Crawley and won – after rejecting his offer of the ladies' tees. It is said that she offended his sense of the golfing proprieties by saying (if it was his honour): 'Your beat, Len'.

In 1953, she underwent a major operation for cancer but came back the next year to win five times and put the opposition to the sword in the US Open by winning by 12 strokes. Even so, the disease was to kill her when a sequence of operations in 1955 and 1956 could not save her life.

FUZZY ZOELLER

Frank Urban Zoeller
(1951–   )
USA, was born in New
Albany, Indiana.
One of the few players in golf
who looks as though he is
enjoying the walk. He won
the Masters in 1979 and the
US Open in 1984.

Fuzzy Zoeller had a slim record in amateur golf – the Florida State Junior College Championship and the Indiana Amateur – when he turned professional. In his first year on Tour, 1975, he won some $7,000 but said he had enjoyed spending about $35,000. But the money soon began to flow in and he attracted considerable press attention during the 1976 Quad Cities event by a round of 63 (a rare feat in itself), which included birdies at each of the last eight holes. This equalled the Tour record.

An annual climb up the money list followed and he passed what was then the good target of $100,000 for the first time in 1978. The following year he began to win and a San Diego Open victory qualified him to play in the Masters. National fame lay just ahead, though at the time only Horton Smith and Gene Sarazen had won on their first appearance at Augusta. That hardly counted as these victories came in the first two events.

Zoeller was hardly noticed during the event, even though he stood 3rd on the US money list at the time. He began with a 70, three off the lead, but after the third round there seemed to be only one winner – Ed Sneed, who was five ahead of his closest pursuers and six better than Fuzzy. Zoeller had been having a steady tournament with rounds of 70, 71 and 69. In the final round he produced more of the same for a 70. He hadn't made anything at all happen till the 8th, a par 5, which he birdied and it wasn't until he birdied the 17th to go to eight under par that anyone thought he had a chance. Even so, it was still very much Sneed's Masters. Zoeller just managed a par on the 18th. Sneed, on the other hand, dropped a stroke to par on each of the last three holes. It was a play-off between Sneed, Zoeller and Watson, the latter everyone's favourite to win.

After all three had their chances of winning birdies on the 10th, the first play-off hole, it was Zoeller who holed from some eight feet on the 11th to win. Even so, Zoeller had been lucky. Playing the 17th in his final round he was four off the lead. He hadn't won (except in the play-off), but Ed Sneed had lost the Masters.

In his next major victory it was a very different story. This was the US Open of 1984 at Winged Foot, the course which had given the players so much trouble back in 1974. Fuzzy opened with a round of 71. There was no limelight but he was tidily placed, three off the lead. After the second round, it looked as though the last Winged Foot champion, Hale Irwin, might do it again. He played a second round of 68; Zoeller, with a fine 66, in which he missed only one green, moved up to his shoulder, one behind. The third day, he was paired with Hale Irwin, and at the end of it the position was little changed. Irwin led by one from Zoeller, with Greg Norman a shot further back.

OPPOSITE: *Fuzzy Zoeller has*
had problems with his back
for most of his career but has
proved able to seize chances
when they come

In the final round, Zoeller produced a string of birdies early on and Irwin was soon out of it, eventually dragging his feet in with a 79. After Zoeller reached the turn in 32, he had a three-stroke lead on Norman. Then came a two-stroke swing to the Australian on the 14th. There was just one in it with four to play. Zoeller dropped a shot on the 17th while Norman managed to work miracles on the last three holes salvaging pars from unlikely positions. This was especially true on the 18th, where Greg hit a good tee shot and then hit a 6-iron sideways into the grandstand. Politely, a spectator caught the ball and, in due course, handed it back. Norman then pitched through the green to about 40 feet from the hole. He had a downhill, swinging putt. No one had ever holed such a monster to tie or win the US Open – but Norman had. Back down the fairway, Fuzzy, thinking Norman had birdied the hole, took a towel from his golf bag and waved it to signal mock surrender. Soon, however, he realised that he would tie if he got a par 4 on the last. He managed it and in the 18-hole play-off Fuzzy seized an important early advantage with a birdie putt of more than 20 yards on the 2nd for a 3. Norman took 6. Zoeller's lead grew and grew and it all finished with a tally of 67 to 75. He had certainly won this championship and been in the heat of contention almost throughout.

Zoeller has been suffering from a back injury right through his golf career and it sometimes seems that he can only hope to play his best when the problem is quiet. Surgery in 1984 certainly helped. The year of 1986 is some evidence of this. Although Fuzzy was only 13th on the money list he won three times. Many others have finished higher without a single victory.

By the end of 1988, Zoeller had ten US Tour wins and nearly $2\frac{1}{2}$ million of prize money. He played on the 1979, 1983 and 1985 Ryder Cup teams.